Crossroads
You Are Here

Crossroads You Are Here

AN EASY, EFFECTIVE GUIDE FOR THE UNFIT, INSECURE & WEARY

MICHELE PAIVA

Copyright © 2002 by Michele Paiva.

Library of Congress Number: 2002091937
ISBN: Hardcover 1-4010-5743-8
Softcover 1-4010-5742-X

All rights reserved. No part of this book may be reproduced or transmitted in any form or by any means, electronic or mechanical, including photocopying, recording, or by any information storage and retrieval system, without permission in writing from the copyright owner.

This book was printed in the United States of America.

To order additional copies of this book, contact:
Xlibris Corporation
1-888-795-4274
www.Xlibris.com
Orders@Xlibris.com

Contents

Acknowledgements 9
Preface 13
Introduction 15
Chapter One
   Getting into Gear 19
Chapter Two
   You Are the Vehicle 29
Chapter Three
   A Personal Crossroad. 32
Chapter Four
   Pack Your Bags!
   (And Then Throw Them Away!) 39
Chapter Five
   Souvenirs 43
Chapter Six
   The Nutritional Crossroad 47
Chapter Seven
   My Nutritional Story 55
Chapter Eight
   Recipes to Fuel You 59
Chapter Nine
   Crossroad—Physical Health 66
Chapter Ten
   My Physical Fitness story 72
Chapter Eleven
   A Fitness Program for Beginners 75

Chapter Twelve
A little Pilates, a little motivation
from trainers around the globe 78
Chapter Thirteen
Crossroad: Relationships 88
Chapter Fourteen
Domestic Abuse 95
Chapter Fifteen
Crossroad: Spirituality 100
Chapter Sixteen
Crossroad: Stress Management 105
    My Own Stress Story... 109
    Ways To Relax 111
Chapter Seventeen
Aromatherapy— 115
Chapter Eighteen
Beauty for Everyone, Naturally 120
    It's the handshake. 126
    Beauty isn't always about looking perfect. 127
Chapter Nineteen
The Ongoing Journey
That We Call "LIFE" ....:.............. 129

DEDICATED TO
MY HUSBAND, STEVE

A PORTION OF THE PROCEEDS OF THIS BOOK
WILL BE DONATED TO THE FAMILY
VIOLENCE PREVENTION FUND

Acknowledgements

I'D LIKE TO thank my wonderful husband, Steve, for being such a supporter and driving influence in every step that I take. Steve, your love surrounds me and keeps me warm when the world can seem cold. You believed in me when I didn't believe in myself. I love you.

To my mother-in-law, "Mom", thank you for being the matriarch of a great, loving family—I fell in love with your son, not realizing that I'd also find love and friendship with your daughters and their families as well. You are the role model for what a "fit, healthy" person should be!

Thank you to the people at Xlibris, for working with me and turning a thought into a reality.

Thank you, Kathy Brinkman, for being a coach who is more than a coach, but a wise teacher of life! Where else could I get information on how to handle intricate, serious situations as well as situations such as where to get "Jammin' clothes"!

Mary Richardson and the International Team— Thank you so much; you have put the crown upon my head and I hold it there with pride. Your organization promotes all things good, all things fair, and I am proud to be affiliated with you.

To Tim Hawthorne, my friend, my mentor. Your professionalism, creativity and varied talents have taught me much, and brought me much joy.

To Dolly at the Chester County Domestic Violence Center, to Tia at the Silent Tears organization and to Noelle at the Family Violence Prevention Fund, for helping me and others to be proactive regarding the prevention and intervention of domestic violence.

Also, a sincere thanks to my agent, Greer Lange, for seeing something in me—finally!

To Dave King, a true friend, confidant and pillar to lean on.

To my workout buddies—always around to cheer me on or jab at me—always welcoming and positive in my life.

To Greg Ladd & my network of trainers all over the globe for your support

To everyone at the studio, regardless of age, you walk through the door and add yourself to the atmosphere.

CROSSROADS
YOU ARE HERE

To all of my friends and family who have brought me life experiences and shared experiences of life, thank you for being there and being a part of my many crossroads.

... and of course, to my children, Alexandria and Nicholas, who are the lights of my life—I love you both and hope that as you grow and continue on in your own journeys, they will be filled with kindness, peace, love and that your souvenirs will be fond memories to treasure.

Preface

I WAS ONCE unfit, insecure, and weary! I looked to books, because I was too insecure to even take a fitness class or join a gym. What I found was that there was a lot of general information out there, but not a lot for those who are or who feel, very unfit. I also noticed that rarely did the books get to the roots of most problems associated with diet and exercise. Negative diet and fitness habits usually stem from insecurity or an accumulation of bad habits that are hard to break if you don't know how. With sadness I will also note that some type of domestic abuse has also touched many of the men and women that carry issues with them through life. Domestic Violence breaks down your overall wellness and your fitness and diet can often suffer because of it.

I wrote this book because I feel that the information I've collected through life, through my own path and that of others has been an ongoing and monumental learning experience. Almost everyone has something in their life, right now, that they would like to change. Many have several aspects of their life that they would change. Unfortunately many don't really know how to do that. I have found that the best path is usually not the easiest path. No one likes the tough road. Everyone also wants the quickest route. I've formulated a series of exercises and mental coaching techniques that can help you to move slowly as not to propel yourself into a crash situation. There are simple, effective and proven ways to achieve results in your goals, regain your spirit, and enjoy your journey.

Introduction

ALONG THE FOLLOWING pages on your travel you are about to embark on, you will see quotations labeled, "Billboards". These are meant to take notice of and think about, just as the billboards on highways are meant to catch your attention. The billboards are just a little extra to get you motivated and thinking.

The note pages at each "Rest Stop" are there to offer a moment for you to regroup, put your thoughts on paper. Refer back to it when you feel that your spirit is broken, or when you feel unmotivated, or that you just are feeling that negativity creeping back.

Billboard, "A man travels the world in search of what he needs, and returns home to find it"

George Moore

Right now, no matter how you feel your life is going, you are essentially at a crossroad. It isn't just someone in crisis that faces a crossroad—or several crossroads. Every minute of every day you are faced with choices. You control your actions and responses to the many stimuli of the outside world.

These choices, actions and responses can be thought of as individual crossroads. Every time you come to a crossroad, you stop, ascertain, and take action—or choose to not take action. Sometimes you proceed and don't think much of it. Most people don't think in terms of "Oh, I am at a crossroad" unless you really are in a crisis or mini-crisis. But, regardless of how often your life decisions are a conscious part of your day, they are still in fact, decisions you are making that do effect your life.

Sometimes you proceed in life and are thrilled at the road you are taking. Things seem to feel like they are "going your way" . . . which is usually the cumulation of a lot of great decisions and outlooks on those little crossroads. Other times, you feel out of control, like you are swerving on an icy road. Sometimes you feel lost, like you are going even the wrong way. Perhaps you have a time in your life, maybe even now, where you feel that you are speeding carelessly through your days—and worst, is when you feel like you are about to have a breakdown.

You are going on a journey but you see that your journey is really within yourself. For a lot of people, as mentioned, those little crossroads we face every day are an afterthought. The breakfast choice you made this morning—or even if you ate—that was a choice, a crossroad . . . those little choices add up. Some of us feel very sure of ourselves most of the time. But guess what—we are still facing crossroads and we need to be aware of what is working and what isn't. Everyone has room for improvement. Some of us are less sure of ourselves and our ability to make decisions. We feel our life paths are a bit rockier and we feel that traveling ahead is a chore. Sometimes we feel like we just want to stop. But stopping is akin to idling. Just existing. Procrastination could be the root, or fear, or a million other reasons or combinations of reasons. Think of it this way. If we don't venture out and come to these crossroads, we never really know what lies ahead in our travels.

Although this book can be a great aid to those in turmoil, such as the case in domestic abuse, it is additionally a benefit and written for the person who wants to simply obtain greater control over or better understanding and increased awareness of their life.

Chapter One

GETTING INTO GEAR

Billboard
"The Journey is the Reward"
Tao Saying

WHEN ONE CHANGES a habit, a series of habits, a goal or an entire lifestyle usually this change needs planning of some sort. Often, if you are not "in" the moment of the goal, new habit or lifestyle, you need to be able to visualize to some extent, what it is you hope to accomplish.

If you are reading this book, you can visualize. Visualization is a form of mental training, and mental training is a form of visualization. The two go hand in hand. When you were young, you probably played games or pretended to be someone or something. This is visualization. Actors and Actresses visualize. Dancers use visualization and mental training when they learn a routine that is challenging, or one in which needs them to get into a character mode. Many time's serious athletes utilize mental training to push themselves farther and to new limits. We all know that many serious athletes have coaches. Some of you may not realize that many serious athletes also have something called a "mental training coach" or, perhaps their coach uses mental training exercises and visualizations to help the athlete obtain greater, more positive results.

Mental training takes focus. You need to have focus in order to achieve most goals. You need to have some kind of a plan, or oftentimes, you will find, the goal gets lost in the shuffle of your life, which can include bad habits, or perhaps they get lost because you are so busy that you have lost focus as to what your goals are.

You need not be ultra creative to achieve a high level of visualization, and you need not be an Olympic hopeful to utilize the mental training techniques that can help you to achieve your goals.

When you were a child, it was fun to pretend. It was fun to daydream and escape the routines of day to day life. As we age, we conform to certain spoken and unspoken rules and guidelines of society and sometimes we become a bit too rigid. We sometimes lose the ability to allow ourselves to take the time to carelessly daydream or to play. We forget that there are myriads of colors, or that texture abounds us. We forget to be silly. In fact, it seems that in the teen years and early twenties, we are just trying to fit in, to calm the child within us to appear more "grown up" . . . and somewhere in the shuffle, we lost a part of ourselves that feels free to be creative.

Some of us did not lose that freedom, but perhaps those "creative types" went to the extreme and lost the ability to focus and persevere. Maybe we spend too much time unleashing our creativity only to find we have spent too many years daydreaming, and too little time in achieving goals.

For instance, for a long distance runner, visualization can play a very important role. After perhaps ten miles, a runner may feel shaky, weak and emotionally and physically depleted. They may feel that they can not go on, that they can barely take another step. Now, someone who is not visualizing, or should I say, visualizing correctly may be thinking and "seeing" something like this in their mind.

> "I can't go on. It's hot. I'm weak. Look at all the people in front of me"

Now, think of what that does to the runner. He is already feeling defeated. He is already "seeing" others "winning". He is going to find it very hard to muster the energy or will to push himself because he doesn't "see" it for himself and is concentrating on the negatives.

Chances are, this runner will not win, as he is running without much spirit, without much motivation. He IS visualizing without even knowing it. He is simply visualizing scenarios and realities that are not in his best interest, therefore, if this is all he is feeling at the moment, it will probably become a self fulfilled prophecy.

Now, let's take another scenario. Same runner, same conditions. It is hot outside, he is weak. There are other runners in front of him.

"I've run this far, look at this. This feels great; my body is being pushed. It won't be long until the people in front of me tire, and I will begin to take the lead, a little at a time."

Now, chances are even if this runner doesn't win, he will come in at a better time than if he were thinking negatively. He probably will because he is showing confidence in himself, he is realizing that although he is hot and weak, that his body is a strong instrument and he is doing well physically all things considered. He also realizes that the people in front of him may slow down, drop out or that his pace may quicken and he could not only catch up, but also surpass them.

Both times the runner was using visualization. Both times the visualization was having an effect on the runner.

I'm sure that almost everyone reading this book has used visualization. Visualization is all those times where you said out loud, or said to yourself, "I bet . . ." or "I hope . . ." It's all those times you got yourself worked up before an event or confrontation, or worked up in any situation (going to the dentist is a common one!). It's also all those times where you did not prepare enough. The bottom line is, many times in our daily life, we have the opportunity to visualize, and though we may, we often do so in a much more uncontrolled, reactive manner.

We need to stress more on proactive visualization. For most of us, we will not have to visualize so intently like a distance runner in a long marathon. For the most part, all we have to worry about is getting through little humps in the road that daily life brings us.

Here is an example of proactive visualization.

Situation: You are going to the dentist, and you have been having pain in and around a tooth for about three days. It's getting worse. All you can think of is that you don't want a root canal, filling, or the tooth pulled. You are imagining pain or just being uncomfortable. Maybe you are worried because you have had bad experiences in the pst. At least two people have told you it would be nothing to worry about. Another person though, had a different story. They had a nightmare story about their cousin having the same symptoms, and it ending up in a root canal that ended up infected a few days later because the dentist didn't clean out the tooth enough. All of this is running through your mind. You are visualizing in a reactive manner. Now, maybe you go to the dentist and you do need a root canal. Even so, he does them several times a day and he pretty much knows what he is doing right? So what are the chances that this routine procedure will go wrong? Almost nil. Now, on the flip side, you could go in and perhaps you only have a particle of food trapped in your gum, and a simple swipe from the dentist or hygienist dislodges the particle, you wash your mouth out and they send you on your way.

Again, here, proactive visualization is the key. No matter what the actual outcome, if you are more positive about the experience you will HAVE a more positive experience because your mindset is in the proactive mode, instead of the reactive.

Being proactive also helps you to retain some control over the situation, which even if you don't think you have, you actually do. It is in your control how you handle any given situation. A reactive person simply reacts on the cuff to stimuli, to situations and interactions; therefore, they are much less in control of most situations, including their own thoughts.

The mental training that we talked about is also very proactive instead of reactive. Visualization is to creative people what Focus is to the steadfast types. In broad generalization, those who are creative usually lack focus, and those who are less creative lack visualization. The trick is to become somewhere in the middle. You need something to get you to visualize in the first place, something to keep you visualizing in a proactive manner, and then, you need something to keep you planning and being proactive in your actions. This is focus. Focus is having a grasp on where you are and where you want to be—and real focus is having a plan to get you there, which should be a combination of visualization, actions and decisions.

Now, let's go back to the runner. He didn't just wake up and run 10 miles without any planning. He didn't just visualize running ten miles for a year then is ready to run a marathon. He had focus. A plan.

Perhaps six out of seven days a week, he ran either on a treadmill or outdoors. He probably did a combination. He may have also done some weight training and some visualization training with his coach. He may have also altered his diet to fit a more athletic lifestyle—which means probably adding more calories in the form of proteins. Even on those days where he had off from work and had the chance to lounge around the house in the morning, he still got up early and worked out. He did not stop running when it was raining, because he knew that not only did he need to continue with his FOCUS but that it's possible that on the day of the marathon it could rain, therefore, he realized it is best to experience all viable conditions. This way, if he does find that if he runs in the rain on the day of the marathon, he can VISUALIZE back to a day and say to himself, "I did this already, I can handle it"—He prepares, he has focus.

Now, let's go back to the more common experience of going to the dentist. This is an easy one. It's what we teach children. It's what you hear on commercials that sell toothpaste. "Brush your teeth!" If you PLAN on brushing your teeth a couple or few times daily, it is probable that you have had enough positive and planned focus that you need not fear going to the dentist because you have, in essence, prepared yourself for a more pleasurable, or at least, comfortable visit. If you have focus, you can be pretty sure that even if you have some tooth pain, that it probably isn't anything real serious—and even if it is, you know that your overall dental health is pretty good, so you will bounce back quickly. You have prepared, you had focus.

In upcoming chapters we will talk about lifestyle nutrition, lifestyle physical fitness . . . . you will see that in each crossroad, a certain level of focus is needed. This means that you can't just jump into a decision. You have to really plan, really put thought into it, and you really have to have focus and commitment. Overall, you will be concentrating on your well being. Your travels are really all about you finding yourself and what works for you. Each crossroad is about you. Your well being is the goal, or focus, of each visualization and crossroad.

Regardless of whether you find yourself on either side of the spectrum of creativity or focus, or if you are somewhere teetering in the middle, you need to begin your journey with an open mind, a clear heart that will seize creative moments, the scenery of life. You will also need to be able to attempt to look at that map and focus on where you are going and where you have been. You need to think if you are ready to grasp the steering wheel and take the drivers seat. If you feel that this is a journey that you can really enjoy the ride, then you are ready to rev yourself up and learn important, yet basic techniques that will help you in your many roads that you will travel.

The following exercises for unleashing creativity may feel silly at first. Allow the silliness to wash itself over you, and allow the part of you that has been silent for so long to surface.

Take some time and listen to music you normally would not . . . perhaps you are not a fan of classical or country . . . or not as familiar. Take time to listen to it. Allow yourself to move to it. Maybe you want to simply listen to lyrics and try to "feel" the words. Maybe you want to listen to the music and simply relish in the many sounds of the instruments—all the highs and lows of the notes . . . and then, think of what the music would look like if it were a painting.

Grab a pencil, a pen, or better yet, a box of crayons or paint. Get yourself some paper—even a small notepad, and just start putting lines and shapes on the paper. Allow yourself to not judge your works of art, but to look at it as fun and a release. Draw, color or paint what sad looks like, then angry, then love. Take feelings and emotions and put them to paper.

After allowing yourself to unleash your creativity, you should get in the habit of doing so. Once is not enough. Make creativity a part of your life. You don't have to be a ballerina or gallery artist, but just allow yourself to express your creative side . . . . and yes, you have one!

Mental training is a bit more technical, a bit more laboring. You may find that you lose concentration or that you need breaks. That is ok—it's all about progress and trying something a little different.

Think of a short-term goal. Concentrate on that goal. Imagine yourself at the finish of the goal . . . now rewind a bit, and think of yourself right now. Now, from start to finish, with details as small as what you are wearing and the sounds around you, begin focusing on how you will achieve that goal. After you have finished, rewind again, now change some factors, and achieve the goal again. Do this several times. Imagine setbacks, imagine resolutions. After a while, it will seem as if you already know how to achieve your goal with little effort or at least, with little surprises or obstacles.

You are now on your way. Your journey is already beginning.

REST STOP

Chapter Two

YOU ARE THE VEHICLE

"We acquire the strength we have overcome",
Ralph Waldo Emerson

WHEN YOU ARE at a crossroad, you need to think of what vehicle you are traveling in. Your decisions will be based greatly on that vehicle. How you feel you look, how you see yourself and what you are physically allowing yourself to accomplish are primary to your decisions in life. You need to identify the vehicle your state of mind is really in. Do you feel you are in a beat-up old car? Do you feel you are in a generic van? A sportscar? A moped? Are you feeling your vehicle is out of fuel? This book uses a lot of imagination techniques. As mentioned, as a creative professional, I've found that those in the arts can portray emotions because of their ability to imagine emotions and feelings. It is also proven that athletes use imaginative focus to gain better control . . . therefore, I want you to apply these same, proven skills to your life, to your journey.

When you are thinking about your vehicle, you need to take serious consideration to it's running condition. What I mean is, are you in sound medical health? This is very important. If you were a race car driver and expected optimal results, you would not take a car out onto the track without knowing if it ran well. The same should be true for your body. Make a commitment to visit your physician and make sure that you are in optimal health—if you are not, take the proper precautions while you are on your journey at all times. If you do not, you will in essence, break down. Heart issues, anemia, even something as small as PMS can effect the decisions you make when you reach crossroads. Perhaps you or a loved one is suffering from an acute or terminal illness, and all the roads ahead look long and baron. You may feel that you are swerving off the road, headed for a crash. This is not a book that will push you to feel that you are failing if you are not happy every minute. That thinking is unrealistic. You will have plenty of hardship if you are faced will critically ill health. It will be hard to look ahead at the map of your life if you honestly know that you may have only months to live. I have not been in that situation personally, but my mother was. She was faced with being told that she had less than a year to live. In her case, but not in all cases by any means, she did live less than a year. But in that year, she taught me about having a strong will and embracing life. You see, I am not trying to teach you something I learned while achieving great success, but something a dying woman taught me, when facing her last days. Hardships are to be expected in the throes of terminal illness or even if you have a serious disease. I'm not saying to suck it up and smile. I'm saying to find something about your situation that you feel you can control. If that situation is that you just need to lower your sugar intake, or if that situation is that you have cancer—the mindset is the same. Find something you can control. Can you control the foods you eat? If you are in a serious hardship situation, can you control some of your thoughts so that you think more often of the happy times and less of the times you feel you regret? It doesn't matter if your journey will last for the next hundred years or the next day—it is still your journey to cherish.

The more in control of your health you are, the better you will feel along the way in your journey.

REST STOP

Chapter Three

A PERSONAL CROSSROAD.

"Have confidence that if you have done a little thing well, you can do a bigger thing well too",
  Storey

YOU NEED A peaceful mindset to really feel comfortable at your crossroads. Think about it—when you are under considerable stress or distracted, you can't always feel comfortable making decisions—and when you are upset—isn't the common advice "wait till you calm down before you make a snap decision" or, "Calm down before you say something you'll regret!" . . . It's because when one is in any type of turmoil, the decisions one makes can be fueled not by always the most logical choices, but by more impulsive emotional choices . . . and once a choice is made, you usually have to either live with it, change it or accept and enjoy it. OK? So,

CROSSROADS
YOU ARE HERE

please take a moment and try to imagine an actual crossroad. Is it a deserted prairie area? Is it a city intersection? Whatever works for you. I like to use as my imaginative crossroad a real crossroad in my hometown. It has beautiful residential homes with manicured front lawns. I imagine it after a summer rain, with everything green and lush.

A lot of people don't always want to come to grips that in order to really achieve self-esteem and confidence, they have to succeed emotionally in all area's of their life. This does not mean you have to succeed at being rich, in love and all of the dreams of a pop culture society! It simply means you have to be able to honestly say that you are really happy in your own skin, and totally confident at your life decisions.

What you will find is that AS you travel through life, and AS you make decisions you feel good about, you will develop that self esteem and confidence that you feel you lack.

Let me also say that within each crossroad, you will have to look not only on the surface, but also within. There will be many who read this book who think their personal lives are perfect, meanwhile, they are really quite dysfunctional. Or perhaps there will be those who are obsessed with weight loss, though they are not overweight. You have to perceive yourself as realistically as you can. You can't look at yourself, as you know yourself. You have to look at yourself as somewhat of an outsider in some ways. If you have low self-esteem, you will feel that you are not as attractive, slim, healthy, successful or in love as perhaps, you really are. Then again, those with over-confidence, those who have built a tough exterior wall to protect themselves will claim that they are completely happy, meanwhile, they may be overweight, unhealthy, or in a dead-end relationship.

The goal here is to really look at yourself without judgement, and take yourself for who you are. You need to come to grips that perhaps you are a bit stocky, and that stocky is "ok". Maybe you are content in your marriage but feeling bored. Maybe the problem isn't your marriage, but that you are bored with yourself, and the marriage is the scapegoat.

Perception is very individual. Everyone has his or her own perception. You will find also, that many people have a lack of self-confidence in at least some area of their life. You will find that as you tell others that you are on a road to self-discovery and improvement, which you are facing your crossroads in a proactive manner instead of reactive, you will get a myriad of responses.

Some responses will be favorable. That's great. The people that are positive will probably be very interested in this for you and even for themselves. This will be your future support system . . . and perhaps your imaginary driving partners at times.

As mentioned, there will be a variety of responses. Some may be mocking. Some may be patronizing. Some may be degrading. The bottom line is, you have to think of this as noise and pollution. You have to be able to tune them out, and not let yourself breathe in their toxic energy. Imagine yourself rolling up your car windows, putting the air on and filtering them out.

Let me give you an example. My mother. She loved me. She wanted the best for me. But I was young, in my teens, and had dreams of being a big-time choreographer. Now, let me preface this with that my mother grew up in the depression era, and at that, lived in an orphanage. Her life, and her perception of life, was very different from my life and my perception of life. So, there I was, telling her that I was going to keep going to dance school and become a choreographer. Here she was with just hoping that I would meet a nice man someday, a nice man with a good job, settle down and have children. She would tell me all kinds of things to discourage me. Now, whether she believed them or not is not the issue. What is the issue is that she wanted me to believe them. She told me that I was being brought up in a rural area, and only people from New York "made it" in entertainment. She told me I wasn't the best dancer at my dance schools anyway, so why did I think I was going to succeed as a "big time choreographer" . . . She even had moments where she told me, "Only pretty girls get jobs like that". (Yet she did often tell me I was attractive, when the stakes were not as high)

Time went by quickly, as it does seem to do when you are young. I moved out, and sure enough, opened a dance studio. I loved to teach dance and wanted it to be my job. I had an independent spirit and wanted to be self-employed. It was wonderful. It wasn't long before my students were entering dance competitions and I loved the thrill of seeing my students compete. I was still young, in my early twenties, so I competed sometimes too. One day, I was asked to be a judge . . . I loved that too. I began networking, long before I knew what "networking" was. Then it happened. I was asked by a fellow judge to go to Philadelphia and choreograph a segment on a locally produced and locally aired television show. But for me, with no television experience and being still in my early twenties, this was in fact, the "big time choreographer" break! I loved it, and my love for my craft must have shown through, because I went on to local, stage and national choreography positions. What did I do that is perhaps different from a kid who becomes easily discouraged and gives up? I learned to focus, be imaginative, and to tune out negativity. That wasn't all. I kept this as my basis for life. I took criticism, and I took advice . . . . but when it became something I realized or felt was overly negative and not proactive, I just took it with a grain of salt. Did my mother's words hurt me? Of course. But can I look back now and see a little bit how those words came to cross her lips? After all, I know she loved me and she was usually very positive. Yes, I can look back and see her as a mother who didn't want her daughter to get crushed feelings. It was her way of discouraging me instead of someone else totally stomping on my dreams. It also showed me that she was afraid for me. She had a very different life than I, and a very different outlook and risk factor than I. I can look back and see that my mother never would have pursued the dream that I did . . . but also, when you stop pursuing dreams, you begin to stop dreaming. I love to dream. The dreams that we can achieve are infinite.

Crossroads
You Are Here

So, although I gave you just a sampling, I think you get my drift here. You need to believe in yourself, even if no one else does.

By the way, after I did "make it", my mother was my biggest supporter. I am lucky to say that. I know that there are many of you who think or know, that your loved ones would not ever be supportive, and that may be true. But that's not what this is about. This isn't about making everyone else happy so that you have fit into his or her little puzzle. It's about you being you. Confidence and self-esteem are going to get you there. If you have any at all inside of you, muster it up. Realize that there are times where you will feel emotionally weak and lack esteem. We all have those moments. If it helps at all, and right now, I do feel very confident in my loved ones, and myself then you must use me as inspiration. If I, a rural country girl from Guthriesville, PA, can go on to what I feel, have been great things, you can too—whatever is great to you, whatever your perception will allow. Here I was, this speck in this little village, and you may feel like just a speck wherever you are. But guess what—we are each so much more than we can ever imagine. Have I been let down? Of course! Do I dwell on it? Really? Yes. I will not say I'm some upbeat person twenty-four hours a day, seven days a week. I'm not trying to "sell you" some unrealistic lifestyle. I have down time, I have a good cry now and then, I get angry, and yes, I make some negative crossroad decisions at times. But I try to concentrate on the positive, and you should too. No one is perfect, and if you try to be, you are setting yourself up for failure, which will erode at your self-esteem. Try for being somewhat confident. See the good in you—because we all have it. There are a lot of crossroads out there. If you look in your rearview mirror, you will see the ones you have already traveled. The beauty of this trip, is that it will continue on, and that you will be choosing your path no matter what the particular road you are on.

It's my job to help you to realize that you have these crossroads and that they all connect to become that wonderful, illustrated and ongoing map that is you!

REST STOP

Chapter Four

PACK YOUR BAGS!

(AND THEN THROW THEM AWAY!)

*Billboard "It takes vision and courage to create,
it takes faith can courage to prove"*
Owen D. Young

BEFORE WE EVEN plan our trip, we have to realistically look at our baggage that you have packed and are carrying around. Now, you are expecting me to start dissecting your baggage, and analyzing it. I am not going to ask you how you feel about the relationship of your mother or ex-wife or if you think your third grade teacher is the reason why you feel this way or that way or act this way or that way. I am going to ask you to realize that all of the extra baggage you carry around is probably really not needed to continue your journey. Think of it. Yes, you may have been really hurt or really wounded as a child. You may have been really angered by your ex-spouse or you best friend. But, take this day, the beginning of your new journey, and accept all of it. Accept that you may have been angered or wounded, and that you are going to probably live tomorrow and the next day. It's just an issue of if you want to live tomorrow and think about the issues of years ago or if you want to just start the journey and make a new day, and another new day, and then it becomes a new month . . . and so on.

So, let's think of the big issues—the ones that bother you the most—as really big ugly luggage. Do you really want to bring ugly luggage filled with heavy stuff on your journey? If not, get rid of it. If you want it, you better wait before you go on your journey—because it isn't going to fit in your vehicle. If you want to hold on to big, ugly issues that fit in big, ugly baggage, then you are not ready for this journey . . . but you can keep reading, and then come back to this point when you are ready to "let go". Only great positive things are going in that vehicle. You would not bring an ugly bathing suit on vacation that will make you feel bad right? You would not bring a fur coat to a beach, right? Some things are useless and some things will only make you feel bad no matter what. It's best to just ditch the bad stuff and make room for the good stuff.

Take this time to use that imaginative focus. Close your eyes but "look" around you. Do you see a lot of baggage? Get rid of it. Imagine a really great little, easily carried bag. This is the only luggage you need. You are going to fill it with lots of great, positive stuff. You are going to fill it with souvenirs from your trip, collecting a souvenir at each crossroad.

One problem is that a lot of us, being animals of emotion, tend to react on emotional impulse, and tend to get caught up in the mess around us. We also tend to want to fix everyone around us . . . . but the "fixing" always tends to make US like THEM more or make THEM more adaptable to US. So, is it really fixing? We need to focus on being more accepting. Now, I am still telling you to THROW OUT THE BAGGAGE, but you can also learn to accept that once you toss the baggage, it will still be there in your little pile of unwanted baggage. If you leave some baggage at home, it will probably be there when you return. One way to deal with baggage is to also be able to keep it and accept it. If it is not horrible baggage, you can keep it. Just don't take it with you EVERYWHERE you go! How many times do you do this? Probably more often than you know—and more often than I'd like to admit for myself.

Here is a great example. I have what I feel is a great marriage to a great man. He is my best friend and all that good stuff. He also can irritate me. (As I him!) SO, when he get's on my last nerve, I tend to carry that around with me. I get in a bad mood, I get more edgy and all that bad stuff . . . normal reactions to stress, to the adrenaline that is building due to stress. So, the proactive thing to do would either be to work out whatever issue I have with him, or to at least do something constructive with this adrenaline, like work out or take a walk . . . but many of us will just mope, get mad, and complain. So, when I do the reactive, what happens is that I am short with my words, less patient, and overall, not exactly a rose to live with. How often have you had an argument with someone and did not let it go? How often did you talk about the event, with the same bitterness, for weeks on end? How often did you get sucked into, or dare I say, start gossip? All of that is just negativity breeding negativity. So, you can see how often we all keep baggage with us. Baggage isn't just people you can choose to ignore. Sometimes, that baggage you have to live with.

Some of us are going to start making excuses. "But my boss is a part of my life now, and is baggage now, so I can't throw that baggage out—because it is still "here"." Wrong. When you change your actions, you change everything that exists in your life. It may take a while, but even your outlook can make all the difference. Maybe, at the end of the journey, you will learn that your boss or whoever isn't really that much of an issue to you. If you think your boss is so much of an issue, perhaps you need to mentally "put that baggage in the closet" and deal with how YOU feel about the baggage itself. For instance, if you have issues with your boss— look at the real stem. If your boss makes you feel inept, then realize if you are or are not really being inept. Maybe if the situation is that bad, you really just need to look for another job entirely. If you are not inept, then just take the negativity from the boss, or others with a grain of salt and focus on yourself and what you already know about you. When you stop focusing on others and start focusing on you—you'll see the difference. You'll learn to make decisions based on you, and that these other relationships will have to adapt to you. Let others come to their own crossroads—yours is just ahead.

Take this time now, to get rid of the baggage!

REST STOP

Chapter Five

SOUVENIRS

*"Experience is a hard teacher because she gives
the test first and the lesson afterwards"*
Vernon Saunders Law

WHEN YOU GET rid of the baggage, save just one bag . . . that is for your souvenirs. At each crossroad of your life, the souvenir is something that you learn, relish, nurture within, downright like, or is good for you. Think of each experience that you have as having some type of "souvenir"—therefore even the not-so-hot journeys will always have a positive light, as long as you can find something positive to keep with you. It's always better to keep something positive within you than something negative. Negativity breeds' negativity, it creates stress, changes your overall outlook and becomes—gasp—baggage!

Sometimes you don't realize that you are picking up souvenirs. Do you have memories that you love to think about? They are souvenirs of your life that you have captured that you relive—much like a snapshot or a postcard of a favorite place. You are going to train yourself to look on the bright side of life. In every experience, you will find a brighter side, a positive light, a souvenir. Something that makes that part of your life, or decision, positive. Turn a bad experience into a positive one by changing your thinking—and it's not as hard to do as you think. It's also not as easy to do as you think either, as you may know! Yes, I'm contradicting myself. That's because thinking with a positive attitude is sometimes a trained habit because not everyone naturally looks at the bright side of life in the face of crisis or negativity.

You all know a whiner. We all can be a whiner ourselves. I can be a whiner. But, you are going to slowly change your attitude by picking up "souvenirs" so that you become less of a whiner! You will stop feeling sorry for yourself, you will stop being a victim, you will stop that entire unproductive behavior, and you will soon see that you have changed your life just by changing your attitude. I'll act as your tour guide, and keep reminding you to pick up those souvenirs . . . . and once you have them, a good idea is to get some post cards and write your souvenirs on paper. Then, you can add souvenirs whenever you think of them. A souvenir can also be any positive thought, or even a compliment or wonderful experience. It's similar to journal writing, but on a much more condensed level. It's all about little blurbs that you write to yourself that you can quickly look at and remind yourself of the wonderful places you've been, so that each crossroad, no matter what the crossroad is, brings a pleasant memory, just like a faded photograph of a treasured friend or vacation memory.

Souvenir: Your first souvenir is one you'll get right now. It's a snapshot of that place you love . . . that crossroad that is welcoming and positive for you. Take out your camera, and take that photo. Look at the photo . . . . hold the photo. Try to get all of your senses involved. What does the crossroads smell like? Mine smells like fresh, clean rain . . . . what does it sound like? I can hear the sound of leaves gently as breeze touches the limbs. Use your senses and really be at the crossroads. Now take that snapshot and put in your bag.

I have quite a few souvenirs that I've collected along the way. I have memories of hugging my mother when she was dying of cancer. It was a special time, and in it's own way, it was beautiful. There was something very peaceful about those last weeks with her that I will always treasure. I have a lot of souvenirs like that. Moments I treasured, emotions I felt, senses that were brought to new levels. I have memories that at the time didn't seem so perfect. I have this memory of being on a family vacation, where both children were a little tired and a little whiney. It was a very hot August day, and it was also far from home. We were outside and eating ice cream. There was no shade to be found, and the kids were on their last legs, and my husband, and I were on our last nerves. But we tried to make the best of it and that moment was soon forgotten, replaced with other moments. But I look back on that day and realize that was a special moment. We were looking at an amazing view in Bar Harbour, Maine, and the kids did love the day. It made me realize that we were pretty lucky to be there, to experience that day at a great place, all of us in health, and all of us together. Little things can be souvenirs. I have awards and certifications, publications . . . but give me a good memory, and that's something I'll really treasure.

This trip is going to be fun. It is going to be creative, even if you are not! All of us can imagine. Those of us who claim to not be creative are wrong. Everyone is creative to an extent. You know all those nights you spend being a worrywart? That's creativity, but negative! Just make it positive! Imagine and seize your creative energy! Motivational. Positive. You see all that baggage? Throw it out! You won't be needing it!

REST STOP

Chapter Six

THE NUTRITIONAL CROSSROAD

Billboard
*"You may be disappointed if you fail, but you
are doomed if you do not try"*
Beverly Sills

Welcome to your first crossroad! I have something great to tell you; unless your doctor puts you on one, don't go on a diet! Diets are temporary. Lifestyles are more permanent. Think of this crossroad as one that has service stations to fuel your vehicle, your body. This is the fuel for the journey—without fuel you really can't go far on your journey, can you? Most of us are lucky enough to not be hungry and we for the most case have the privilege to go to the store and have a wide variety of foods to choose from. Unfortunately, many of us overeat or eat the wrong foods—which is like putting the wrong fuel into a vehicle . . . it may still run, but it won't run well.

Even more common is those of us who do try to eat the correct foods, but then we sabotage ourselves with overindulging the empty calories and vitamin and mineral zapping foods and beverages such as too much caffeine or too many sweets.

We also have the people who are dieting on the yo-yo diet plans or those who don't eat enough of the correct foods. First of all, as mentioned, a diet is usually temporary. Unless you are prepared to live your entire life by the book of some gimmick, then you should not diet. Most diets are unrealistic. You may lose weight of course, but only while on specific guidelines. When you stop the "diet" the weight comes back. Why? Because your body is losing weight no matter what diet when you cut any or all of the following—fat, carbohydrates, calories, liquids . . . . but, how often can we really say we will never eat a carbohydrate again? Puh-leeeeeaase! If you want a real change, get real. Yo-yo dieting will only make your body grab the weight that was lost, hold on to it for dear life, then because of that hold, add a bit more for cushion.and you know that literally, you may get a bit of extra cushion!

So, our first step in this crossroad is to assess your actual fuel intake. Remember, food is really fuel. It's not really there as a comfort or any other psychological reason—but for fuel purposes only. Think of food as the fuel that keeps your body running smoothly.

Factors such as stress, general health, and age do factor into what your true nutritional needs are. The best bet is to speak to your physician or a nutritionist about your needs and how to fit them into your lifestyle. For the average adult, a diet high in fiber and low in fat is a good rule. Fiber can take the forms of fruits and vegetables. Make sure you get protein too with lean meats, fish and poultry. Carbohydrates tend to pack on pounds and turn to sugars—so you want to keep them at a minimal, which means smaller and less frequent servings of pasta, breads and cereals. Remember that vegetables are carbohydrates, so you will get plenty of them with a high vegetarian diet! Cottage cheese is also a carbohydrate and high in protein.

Switch to healthier snacks—and drink more water! Drink at least 8 glasses of water a day—more if you are active . . . . and again, you really need to check with a medical professional to assess your diet. Sometimes just calling your physician's office and speaking to a nurse can help you assess your diet if you don't have any other health issues.

Here you are at your nutritional crossroad. How do you feel about nutrition? If it seems overwhelming to change your overall diet (and it can be!) change just one aspect at a time—remember that this is a positive choice, so make it positive every step of the way. Maybe instead of the three heavy, unhealthy meals and all those junky snacks and empty calorie beverages, you can exchange one unhealthy snack and beverage for a healthy vegetable snack and water. Then, in a couple days, adapt a meal—maybe with less salt, less creamy gravy, less high fat side dishes, no butter and no white bread. Maybe also make that meal a little smaller, as in, healthier portions. If you keep making little healthy changes over the course of a month or two, it won't be such a shock to your body and mind. Eating is fuel. Eating habits are a different story. Eating habits are usually stemmed from psychological issues—for example, eating out of boredom, random "picking" around, munching here and there out of nervous energy (stress) . . . so, the sooner you start to change those habits—a little at a time, the sooner you will see that you are gaining healthy habits. Pretty soon, you'll realize that you don't have to "think' about eating healthy—that is just "happens" just the way the bad habits did! Sometimes people go on diet programs, some are good and some are unhealthy. Even the good ones though, to me, are unrealistic. No one really count's or weighs food—no one can honestly say that doing a mini-algebra or chemistry lesson before each meal when they try to find the numbers of a teaspoon of mustard and it's accompanying ham sandwich—is realistic. It's better to just have good eating habits so that you don't have to do all of that—because in reality, unless you want to count points, weigh food or carry around a flashcard or food wheel for the rest of your life, everywhere you go, it isn't going to work. The bottom line is that most of us know what healthy eating is, and its just willpower to follow a healthy eating lifestyle. Changing your diet a bit at a time is realistic, and as with any goal in any area of your life, don't get distraught over minor setbacks. I mean, if you are doing great, cutting out one junky snack in a day and replacing it with a healthy snack, then don't get bummed if for a day or two, you go back to the old habit. Just sort of think, "yes I did fall back into an old habit, but it's not the end of the world and I will eat healthy my next meal or snack". One thing I've found that works for me is to not say to myself, "I'll start again tomorrow" . . . no—that's called procrastination or dealmaking with yourself. It usually doesn't work, and then if you don't follow through, you feel guilty. Make the change the next meal or snack. If you "fall off the wagon" then make sure the next thing to go into your mouth is healthy. If you just had a fattening cookie snack, then the next meal or snack better be healthy. Do that for yourself. Then, you won't feel guilty, and you've still gotten in that good habit for the day—therefore, you have still reached your goal. Think of it this way. If you've been working on a healthy diet change for a month—you maybe have about 30-60 good changes you've already made. Now, even if you had 10 setbacks, look at how many good changes you've had that you would not have had in that month! Good for you!

Another thing about goals and nutritional lifestyle. I still do eat empty calories. I will still have a bit of ice cream or a slice of cake but I don't eat a ton of ice cream or even always the whole slice of cake. I have enough to feel like, "wow that was good" but that's it. If you eat half of what you normally do in terms of junk, just as a start, you will realize that you do have control, and the sweets or other empty calories you intake become less and less important. I'll be honest—when I first started cutting out the amount of junk I took in, it was a shock to my body. I felt like if I did not eat chocolate I would starve! My stomach would rumble and my mouth would really water for something junky . . . a cupcake or something! But, as I got over that hump, I realized that it was more the power of my bad habits causing those reactions—and once I changed the habits, I was not feeling those desperate cravings! It is hard. It is a choice though—and if you are willing to take babysteps to get to that goal, you will be more in control, and you will gain confidence through your own empowerment with nutrition.

The following page has an area to help you assess your feelings on nutrition. This, in combination with your medical professional's guidelines, will help you to really know yourself better in terms of your realistic nutritional needs.

When did you first realize that you did not eat as healthy as you could?

When did you first really develop poor eating habits?

What do you think is your biggest nutritional downfall?

Do you remember a time when you felt good and perhaps looked better because of a healthier nutritional lifestyle?

Why do you think you were eating healthier at that time?

Do you know people in similar situations that do in fact, eat healthier and perhaps look better?

Do you use crutches as excuses? For example, do you really believe that your metabolism changed after children or age, or that age or your job is your excuse for your poor eating or nutritional habits? (*We will get into metabolism in the next chapter. This said, metabolism changes only if you have a true thyroid issue or lifestyle change which slows it or speeds it up—for most people, you can change metabolism)

What is your long-term nutritional goal—make it realistic. Make it a goal that will take one year.

What small goals can you begin now?

Name 12 goals at least. Be specific. One goal for each month. Please make the goal small enough that you can easily reach it—challenge yourself when you readily reach accomplishments, and don't beat yourself up if you don't. You may add more if you feel confident. You can have up to 24 goals—two for each month. More than that just gets too confusing!

If you don't reach your goal, how far do you want to come to it that would be acceptable?

If you have a setback, what is something you will tell yourself that will keep you motivated and happy.

Souvenir: Imagine yourself eating healthy, fuel-packed foods and beverages. Imagine yourself having more energy and less overall fat, cholesterol and empty calories. Imagine your body processing the protein rich foods and growing stronger!

REST STOP

Chapter Seven

MY NUTRITIONAL STORY

Billboard
*"Habit is habit, and not to be flung out
the window by any man but coaxed
downstairs one step at a time"*
Mark Twain

I'VE INCLUDED A short bio on my own nutritional journey of where I've been—it has not been always pleasant, but you'll see how I did also, like you perhaps, have to overcome nutritional crossroads.

As a kid, my mother made a lot of wonderful dinners—lots of big Italian dinners and lots of focus on healthy eating too. She always had snack food around—not just carrots and healthy snacks, but also ice cream, cupcakes, cakes of all sorts and chocolate.

I grew up being very involved in dance and was very active. I ate what I wanted and was fairly thin. I ate healthy meals and snacks but plenty of junkfood and sodas too! I got older, got married and had children. My lifestyle changed a bit. I was less active in the "whole body" physical sense as in dance, but more active as I was finding myself working, running around doing food shopping, errands and all that goes with raising a baby. I did more prepackaged foods and fast food. I did not lose all of the weight I had from the pregnancy because I really felt great when I lost the first 20 pounds—I was still maybe 15 pounds over my prepregnancy weight, but I did not really work hard at losing it. So, it stayed. I got used to it. I had less sleep because I was up with the baby, and after she would sleep I would grab a late night snack and watch a little TV. After time, I was just less active. I had another child and kept on another 10—so now I was 25 pounds over what I normally was. I still ate a lot of junkfood—and being young and not having as much income, I bought more of the cheaper prepackaged foods and of course, most have less nutritional content but plenty of filling carbs and empty calories.

I found myself years later feeling a bit bored. I had changed my lifestyle because of being a mother and being home was not for me. The kids were in school but I spent my days taking care of the house, doing errands, laundry, shopping and dinners. I had more time to munch as the kitchen and snacks were right there. A few glasses of lemonade a day was refreshing, but also filled with empty calories. A few years later, I went through a divorce and the same time my mother was dying. I felt depressed yet kept plugging along. I would be upset and eat just out of nervous energy, just for something to do, and it tasted good therefore I felt good. The pounds crept on . . . about 10 more. Now, in looking back, let me tell you that almost every step along the way I was at a crossroad at the time (I just didn't realize it). I made the choice to not get in shape again after the pregnancies; I made the choice to eat unhealthy all those late nights with babies and toddlers finally sleeping next to me. I made the choice to eat when I was feeling low instead of maybe talking to others or reading a book, or finding a hobby—or, eating something healthy (which is better when you are under stress, since stress zaps the body!) But then, I realized I wanted to look better and feel better. This was a crossroad I knew I came to. I began to change my eating habits among other things, such as increase my fitness level—which we will get into at the next crossroad—and in time, almost a year, I was actually a healthier eater. I lost 10 pounds without even trying, just by cutting down on junkfood. Now, that 10 pounds came off over time—I am guessing about 8 months. But it came off. I did not even plan for that. Now, I am making the attempt to not only eat healthier, but also eat better portions and tailor my eating for more fuel. I realize that white bread, although yummy, does nothing positive for my body. It turns to sugar and just sort of sits there—becoming extra calories I don't need thus becoming fat on my body. I'm changing in baby steps, because too big of a change will make me feel like giving up. Especially since I'm conditioned to eating certain ways—it will feel like punishment if I change too much. I'm at my own nutritional crossroad with you.

Enjoy yourself. Begin your journey by taking a course of action, by traveling onward. Be your own inspiration. Don't let fear get to you. Don't let the baggage you threw out bother you. This is you, your body. This is your crossroad. Get a friend involved. Find a support person or a support team. If someone on your support team has a setback or falls off the road, you still keep going on that journey!

You are ready for your next crossroad! This is an exciting journey that you have embarked upon!

Souvenir

Imagine that you know me—I am an acquaintance that has just told you the story of my nutritional crossroad . . . now; imagine that you are telling me your story of your nutritional crossroad. What is your happy ending? How will you reach it? Imagine me telling you how wonderful it is that you are getting the courage and willpower to break those bad habits and emphasize your great habits.

REST STOP

Chapter·Eight

RECIPES TO FUEL YOU

Billboard
"Imagination is the eye of the soul"
Joseph Joubert

As A PERSONAL trainer and nutritionist, I have found that most people do try to consume a diet that is fairly healthy. The problem is that a lot of these people don't stop there—they continue and think that because they have had a healthy meal or supplement, it gives them freedom to eat a host of unhealthy foods. For instance, you can't pop garlic pills, or eat a lot of garlic, then eat tons of cupcakes and buttery pastries and assume that you are going to have a great cholesterol reading. So, I've compiled some recipes that should do two things... one, they will help to satisfy your sweet tooth and two, they will help to satisfy your craving for carbs. (In my experience, these are two of the biggest culprits of overeating—craving sweets, craving carbs)

First of all, remember that you are better off—even emotionally in regards to eating—if you eat several small meals a day. It makes sense that the larger meals are in the earlier part of the day, so that they can burn throughout the day, instead of sitting in your stomach all evening. Realistically, most people will not have breakfast as they're largest meal—but if you can, wonderful! This is not to say that you are off the hook from eating breakfast at all. You should have breakfast. It's the meal that really does fuel you. Your body wants it! Your schedule may not like it, your habits may fight it, but your body craves it!

I've compiled a small list of what I feel are realistic meals for you to try.

Breakfast

Egg-Tofu Scramble

Chop onions, peppers, mushrooms and other egg-friendly veggies and sauté them in a non-stick frying pan. In all honesty, on most mornings I have time to just chop an onion. If you can do the chopping the night before and just refrigerate your ingredients, that's great. Add some chopped tofu (any kind) and either an egg or egg substitute and scramble till the egg is done. Add spices if you like, though in the AM, I'm in the mood for more serene tastes, so I stay with the old basic of ground pepper.

Oatmeal w/ fruit

OK—this is about as easy as it can get, it's good for you and you can have a variety of tastes. I prefer the non-instant oatmeal, but if time is an issue, the instant is ok to start with. Just heat water, add oatmeal and add the fruit of your choice. I like to add bananas because they are filling and packed with potassium, which is something that you should replenish in your body daily.

Fruit and Cottage Cheese

This is a great combo. Just add a few tablespoons of cottage cheese to your fruit platter. Cottage cheese has a ton of protein and the fruit adds the zip, fiber and vitamin C, along with anti-oxidants!

Bacon and/or sausage with Eggs with tomato

Now, just because I'm saying bacon and sausage, it does not mean that you should eat half a pound of it. A couple of links of breakfast sausage, and a couple of strips of bacon are enough! You want the flavor and a taste of the meats, not the meats as a side dish or entrée! You can allot up to three eggs per serving if you like.

Heat a pan and cook bacon and sausage till cooked through. Set the bacon and/or sausage aside on a plate lined with paper towels to absorb extra grease. Pour most drippings out of pan, keeping some just to keep eggs from sticking. In a separate bowl, beat eggs with fork will mixed well. Slowly pour onto pan. Keep on medium or medium low heat, so that eggs cook slowly. As the egg begins to cook, add broken up bacon pieces and crumbled sausage to pan. Add a handful of cheese of your choice, sprinkled evenly throughout. Add sliced tomato's, in an even layer. Add a touch of oregano, a touch of basil and pepper to your liking. Cover and cook till egg is done. This is a delicious meal, but you need to remember to have a healthy portion, not a giant portion!

Lunch

Tuna and Spinach Salad

Grab a handful or so of any greens—I prefer baby spinach—add a can of tuna, or half a can. Season with dill, a splash of olive oil and a dash of balsamic vinegar. You can add other veggies, hard-boiled eggs, croutons—whatever you choose.

Veggie Wraps

Make a mix of veggies, cut up small, spinach or other greens, a sprinkle of your favorite shredded cheese and put in center of a soft tortilla. Add a dollop of yogurt, a bit of spices if you like (Mexican spices work well with this) and wrap and eat! This is healthy, delicious and full of anti-oxidants.

Dinner

Tuna Steaks with Pasta

Add zip and health to your pasta dishes. Toss the pasta (any type) with a bit of olive oil. Cut a tuna steaks into chunks—Sauté or grill till cooked. Just when they are finished, add a combination of chopped Greek olives, onions, and roasted peppers. When heated through, toss with pasta. Be sure that you are actually eating more of the tuna than the pasta—a pound of pasta calls for at least two pounds of tuna. If you are cooking for less, or for one, just cook a handful of pasta for a half-pound of tuna.

Lentil Salad with Spinach

Cook lentils till tender. Add a teaspoon of Olive oil, a teaspoon of mustard or a pinch of ground mustard, a red onion, chopped—and toss. If you like, you can add chopped celery and chopped asparagus too. Add a dash of Balsamic Vinegar to taste. Put about a half a cup or cup full as the topping on a warmed spinach salad. This is extremely healthy and filling.

Summer Soup

A great soup that doubles as a meal on those hot days. Blend a small package of silken tofu with about 2-3 very ripe, crushed bananas. Add skim milk till you reach the desired consistency. Add a dash of nutmeg or a dash of pumpkin spice. If you like, dress it up with a topping of dried coconut! You can also make this recipe with plain or vanilla yogurt instead of tofu. This is delicious and also, a very healthy, filling meal.

With all meals, add fruit or extra salad. Try to only

eat breads in the morning or at lunch—or minimally at dinner . . . of course, if you go out to eat, you don't have to deny yourself . . . but if you make small changes during most days, you won't feel guilty when you do have the breads. Usually, now, when I eat breads in the evening I just feel bloated, so I really don't feel so much like I'm missing anything when I pass on the bread helpings!

One thing you need to do is have plenty of snacks—which should be fruits and veggies for the most part. Of course, I won't lie—there are times where I do reach for more than my share of cookies as a snack, but for the most part, I do eat healthy. As far as drinks, you should drink as much water as you can. With your meals, add a squirt or dash of lemon juice, limejuice, or a splash of cranberry juice.

I keep my caffeine to a minimum these days, and so should you unless your physician says otherwise. I do drink two cups of coffee a day, and I do once in a while have a cup after dinner. If you need to destress, (which most of us do) watch your caffeine intake!

I also have a juicer, and it's wonderful. Though, many times with juicing you lose the fiber benefits of the fruit or vegetables, so if you ask me, you need to make sure it's supplemental, not a substitute for eating. It gives you a bang for your buck of vitamins. I can juice a small bag of carrots and drink it in one eight ounce glass . . . that is a lot of antioxidants . . . but watch out, because it's also a lot of sugars. Too much of anything is not good.

When it comes down to it, really it's all about variety and moderation, so no matter what your culture or traditions are in terms of eating, just try to make little steps at eating healthier and keeping properly hydrated.

REST STOP

Chapter Nine

CROSSROAD—PHYSICAL HEALTH

Billboard
"All human activity is prompted by desire"
Bertrand Russell

THIS IS THE crossroad that a lot of people make excuses about. This is where you hear the excuses such as "I don't have time to exercise" "I do exercise and it doesn't do anything anyway" and "I can't afford to buy the equipment or go to a gym" among other crutches!

First of all, let's get this straight. If you really don't want to make a change here, you probably won't. Reading this chapter will not convince you to change your physical level of activity. It will only inspire you. Yes, the Nutritional Crossroad is not easy for some, but one thing is, it doesn't actually cause you to expend MORE energy. Eating right is sometimes a challenge, but it actually will give you energy. This is how the Physical Health Crossroad differs. Now, you are in a crossroad that you actually have to "do" something about. You actually have to make this happen for yourself. You can't just omit something—you have to add it—and that can be very hard for some people—in fact, this might just be the most overwhelming crossroad for a lot of us!

First, you have to assess if you are eating right—or at least embarking on a healthy eating lifestyle. Second, you have to take a good look at this vehicle you call your body. This is where you really also need to check with your mechanic—which is really your physician—to assess how much exercise is enough or too much. One of the biggest mistakes people tend to make when starting an exercise program is overdoing it. They hear that you should exercise 20-30 minutes three times a week, and sometimes dig right into that. Well, if you have been fairly inactive, that might be too much—or it might be just right, but it might discourage you because it may be either too much of a challenge, or too much of a change in lifestyle. Remember that the biggest challenges are because they alter your lifestyle, or habits—not because of what they really are.

So, let's pretend that you are inactive. Inactive does not mean lazy. Inactive in the sense we are speaking of means that you don't, as work or hobby, do anything that raises your heart rate throughout the day. Unless you have a very physical job or hobby where you raise your heart rate often, you are not really "active". Just because a job is not a "desk" job, does not mean you are "active". It means you are not sitting per say, that's all. And if you have what is known as a "desk job" and you work your cardiovascular system less than three times per week, then you should consider yourself inactive as well. If you are inactive, you are going through your journey in a vehicle that although may be properly fueled, it is not really inspected or tuned up. It's not running at its peak. You need to get into the shop for a realignment that is for sure! Especially if you have some problems such as a bad back or bum knee. Most injuries are not caused by the exact injury itself—but usually because the muscle group has not been worked, flexed, stretched and strong—therefore, any minor injury becomes a painful one—where some people would not have had that weak area therefore not have been injured. Understand? No? Let me show you an example. Miss Jones complains of a bad back. She is 65 years old. She has not done much exercise in the past 10 years. Perhaps 15 or 30 years. She moves and "throws her back out" when she is cleaning her home. Her answer is to live with painkillers, heating pads and a special little pillow while she watches TV. She doesn't want to exercise because it means she will be moving her back, therefore she thinks she will be hurting herself. She chalks the injury up to age. She finally goes to the doctor, and he recommends a physical therapist. The Physical Therapist gets her to move more . . . he does simple exercises and she begins to feel a little better. After several weeks, she stops going—and though she feels a bit better, she tells people that she has a "weak" back and that it's from "an injury".

Now, let's change this a bit. Miss Jones does still clean and throw her back out. But instead of the mental process of "I'm old and out of shape" she realizes "Wow, I must need to exercise. My back must be weak". So, in addition to seeing her physician and getting checked, and perhaps in addition to the physical therapist, she also asks one or both medical professionals if she can begin very light exercise. She starts walking more. She starts more back muscle building exercises (just a few at first, because it is a challenge) such as crunches and side stretches. She perhaps takes a swimming class if her finance allows and also a senior's fitness class. If she can't afford it, she calls local gyms and Y's and inquires what they have available for people with a limited income. As she begins to strengthen her back, she feels better. As she feels better, she increases, instead of stops, her physical challenges. She may stop the physical therapist of course—but her home workout continues. She realizes that she doesn't have a weak back at all, and feels better than she has in years.

Now—here is a really alternative take on Miss Jones. Miss Jones works her body out at least three times per week. She knows that the abs and back are tough areas and she wants to make sure to target those areas. She wonders why she doesn't feel the way her friends do. She has adapted fitness into her life and can't see how her friends, who complain about aches and pains, don't do so also.

So—there you have it. Now, it's not to say that if you exercise you won't get a strain or ache—they still happen—but you are more aware of your body and you are really less prone to any serious injury if you do take care of that body. As in a vehicle, it's less likely to be off balance if you get the tires rotated, right? So, you need preventative care for your body, your only real vehicle, as well.

If you are very inactive, you should start with some walking, or arm exercises, which are moderate in speed. Do so for about 5-10 minutes, three times a week. It is not only to not shock your body, but to incorporate fitness into your lifestyle, as to not shock yourself with a new "habit"! As you feel more comfortable with the body and mindset of this commitment, you should gradually add a few minutes each time. Work up to at least 30 minutes of activity (which can be varied) at least three times per week. A great thing, if you can physically do so, is to walk more, and at a brisker pace. These 30 minutes can also include a lifestyle change of parking your car at farther entrances and walking a greater distance. Let someone who is not as in shape or energetic get that close parking spot! Also, walking in a mall is wonderful because you can usually find other walkers too . . . many malls have walking clubs, you may want to check that out. It's free, it's indoors, and it can be pretty uplifting, as you won't be alone.

Don't forget that you should add a bit of weight training. This doesn't mean you have to join a gym. You can do a few sit-ups, adapted push-ups, or arm raises with something in your hands. Anything that is above the norm for you will give your muscles a wake-up call, and to boot, it's good for your bones too.

If you feel you have a pretty good, active lifestyle, you may need to assess it. Maybe you are in a rut. Do you need to build more muscle? Are you too comfortable with your cardio routine? This crossroad is the time you really need to take a good look at yourself and what you are doing. Maybe running is something you love, but it's killing your knees. Make small changes—because even those of us who workout, like our routines and yes, get in ruts.

The point of dealing with this physical crossroad is not only to burn calories and build muscle. You need to also see that exercise has many benefits, from lowering blood pressure, enhancing mood, creating balance and more. Most people benefit from a more varied lifestyle. For instance, I just started Yoga—which is very different for me—but I do like it. I do see benefits and I do like the difference it provides in my body and mind. I teach kickboxing and pilates, and I also go to the gym a few times a week to run, walk briskly and to do light weight training. This may be more than what most people want to do—or less—but this is what works for me and what I have incorporated into my lifestyle. Now, if you read the last chapter, you can probably guess this wasn't the way it always was. I had several years where I did NOTHING. Nothing at all. I was much more flabby, much more tired, and felt basically, "blah". I'm not working out to look like a bikini model, I'm simply working out to feel better first, then to look better too.

REST STOP

Chapter Ten

MY PHYSICAL FITNESS STORY

FOR ME, WORKING out became something to do, because I was having panic attacks and feeling very tense. I was grinding my teeth and just feeling out of shape on top of all of it, which was making me feel washed up. I spoke to my physician and they encouraged me to start working out and actually—to take yoga for stress. I started by joining a gym. And guess what—the first time I visited that gym was six months later! For me, like a lot of people who are not accustomed to working out, fitting fitness into my life was not only a chore, but also a hassle. I had to give up TV time. I had to give up a lot it seemed! The deal is, you have to make it a part of your lifestyle, not a chore. This will take time!

I did go to the gym of course, a few times when I first joined—then, I never seemed to "have the time" or "didn't feel up to it" or whatever. Then, the crossroad hit. I think I just was at that point—that second that I can't recount—where I decided that enough was enough. I started small... I remember getting on the one cardio machine and only being able to stay on it for 8 minutes. My heart was pumping and I felt overworked. I was depressed because I could see that the person next to me was on their machine, the electronic read-out (the timer) on the machine said 24 MINUTES. I'll never forget that day. Here I was huffing and puffing, and this person was already on the machine for 24 minutes, and leisurely speaking, not exerting at all! And the woman looked more out of shape than me, and she was older than me by at least 15 years. But I still went the next day, and with a lot of courage, got back on the machine. It took me about a month to work up to 15 minutes. Then, all of a sudden, I was able to do 30 minutes, brisk, on that machine. After that—I knew I did not have to feel ashamed or insecure... I knew that with training, dedication and taking things slow, I could reach goals... and so can you.

To better understand what your goals are and to better accommodate those goals, please answer the following questions.

What time of day do you feel most energized?

Do you think that you could incorporate at least 5 minutes more (even if that means only 5 minutes) of some type of physical expenditure? This could be in the form of stretching or cardiovascular exercise.

Can you think of three times in the next month (if you are very inactive) or in the next week (if you are semi or very active) that you can add cardiovascular activity to your life? This can be as little as 5-10 minutes each if you are inactive, and 45 minutes if you are active.

What goals do you want to accomplish in your physical crossroad? Is it health, looks or a combination of both?

Will you be crossing this road alone or will you also be hoping (but NOT depending upon) someone else? (Working out, at least to start, is usually easier with a friend).

*You will have to commit that even if your friend makes excuses, you don't fall into the trap.

Souvenir: Imagine yourself stronger, healthier and with more energy. Think of something you would love to do but think you are too unfit to participate in. Tennis? Dance? Walking with friends? Hiking? Now imagine yourself doing the things you wish you could do. Imagine how it feels to accomplish the goals, and to make this a part of your life, not a chore! Imagine doing forms of exercise and enjoying yourself—and realizing that there are challenges, and embracing those challenges.

Chapter Eleven

A FITNESS PROGRAM FOR BEGINNERS

If YOU ARE a beginner, you need to really assess your actual physical level before you begin any program. You should also take serious consideration to your physical level if you are over 30 and have not exercised in a few years.

After checking with your physician, ask him to approve the following regiment for you—or to adapt it to your level (you may need less, you made need more of a challenge)

Cardio—walk for about 10 minutes at a brisk pace for you. Don't compare yourself to anyone; just know what is brisk for you. Make sure you have good sneakers or walking shoes on and proper clothing. If you are getting out of breath, slow down. If it is feeling too much like a stroll, step it up.

Toning—You don't have to do any heavy lifting. Just pick up a few cans in your hand and move slowly . . . bring your arms up over your head and gently touch the cans. Lower your arms gently. Continue this several times.

Try to do a few sit-ups. Make sure you are just doing crunches, where your head does not go all the way up to your knees. You are just trying to contract the abdominals, not impress anyone.

Sit down and also make sure you STRETCH. Even if you are sitting on the couch, lift your legs around, stretch your arms . . . stretch to the point of pulling, not pain. You should always try to be as flexible as you can.It's healthy for your muscles to not be tight. You will get less strained or pulled muscles if you have flexibility in them.

Now, this is a workout for someone who has not worked out and is considered unfit. If you are more fit, then you should really go to your local YMCA or Gym and speak to a personal trainer and begin a workout. If you need to, even walking with friends or jogging is a way to get started, but the bottom line is, get started. Muscles that you don't use will atrophy. Muscles that you do use not only keep everything tone, but also burn more calories all the time. How's that for motivation for toning? Do it for your body and for your ego, if that is a motivator! Regardless, this is your road, and you are traveling it—do you want to be stalling out, or do you want to know you can go for miles? Perhaps you can write down some things to get more active, to get stronger and more flexible.

REST STOP

Chapter Twelve

A LITTLE PILATES,

A LITTLE MOTIVATION

FROM TRAINERS AROUND

THE GLOBE . . .

Billboard
"If it's moving, it's alive"
Unknown

AS A PERSONAL trainer, certified pilates instructor and dance instructor/choreographer, I cannot say enough wonderful things about Pilates. Pilates has helped numerous clients of mine regain strength and control over their bodies. For the most part, I have a generally healthy bunch of clients that I work with who are fairly fit or at least not completely sedentary. I do have quite a few students who have had or have severe back issues, kidney problems, neck pain and so on. I have people who have never exercised or who have not done so in years. I have clients with muscular disease and heart disease. I can tell you one thing. Pilates is the technique for you if you are very healthy and fit, or if you are very unfit. It's a technique for every body.

Pilates was developed by a man by the name of Joe Pilates. I can dedicate an entire book to this mans accomplishments with his technique and how many people this technique benefited, but I'll make a long story short. Joseph Pilates developed a series of manipulations that were designed to aid injured soldiers regain strength. All of the exercises were done from a hospital bed, hence the fact that now in this day and age, what we know as Pilates is a mat-based exercise. Because with all exercise, those who were ill or injured and began their movements with Joseph Pilates began to increase not only muscle tone, but also their overall health improved. It was then realized that the combination of stretching along with the muscle building increased physical health as well as being a great stress reducer and immunity booster!

Soon, athletes and dancers began to learn about this amazing man who developed a series of detailed, formatted exercises, and soon, people from all over the world saw "Pilates" as a standard of exercise.

Years have gone by now—

Regardless of what exercise or sport you take part in, you should try to adapt at least some of Pilates methods.

I personally have developed what I call "PaivaLates" which is a combination of my background in dance, pilates, and various forms of fitness and wellness techniques. I concentrate on strength, flexibility and quantity. It will help to keep you strong—including keeping your bones stronger. Flexibility is important because the more flexible you are, the less chance of pulling something you have. A limber body will even fall more gracefully than a rigid, tight one! Lastly, I do go for quantity. I push my clients to do not 100 Accordions, but 101. If form is good, the quantity helps muscles to "remember" what they are doing and also, it makes for a bit faster of a heart rate. I have some clients that come to me just for Paivalates or Pilates, and I know they are not getting much cardio anywhere. I feel obligated to raise their heart rate a bit, so that they can have a more "whole body" health. Everything should be strong—including the heart! I feel I take the best of various forms, and combine them for my clients—and for you.

Some exercises are traditional to pilates or ballet, with small differences here and there. Try them and enjoy them. Make a goal of doing them every other day. Here are three of my favorite movements.

The Accordion Contraction (Pilates calls a version of this The Hundred)

Lie on your back and feel your spine touching the floor. You may use a mat or put a towel under your back for comfort.

You want to really think about keeping your abdominal muscles pulled in tight, as well as contracting your buttocks. Everything should feel "tight". Have your legs bent, as pictured. You will want to bring your chin to your chest as much as you can. Allow your arms to go to your sides.... Don't think of the movement as a crunch, but as a contraction. You will slowly contract your abdomen and allow your body to curl upward. You only have to curl up a little bit for a nice contraction. As you roll down, allow your body to release, just as an accordion that is opening does. Allow the release until you are again, flat on your back.

Beginners usually do about 30 of these. Advanced students can do several hundred, and with a higher curl. Do what you can, do them daily! You will see improvements in your strength, and possible see inches in decreased size as you firm and tone.

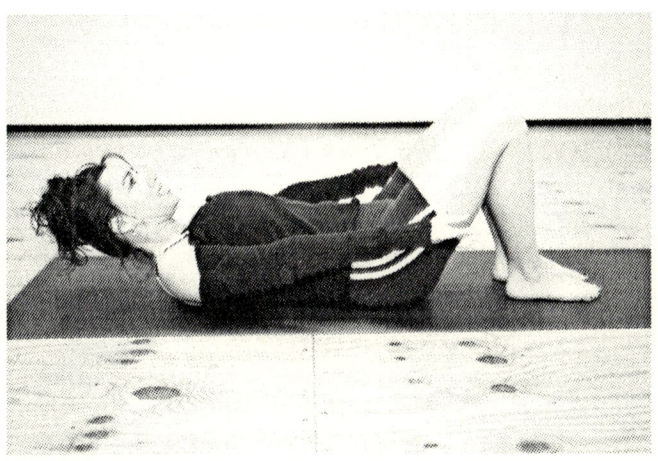

Curl upward
Lower and repeat

The Lying Down Develop

Classical dancers do this amazing step that I've adapted for a floor-based workout. It's the same concept—to develop the leg. It also helps rotate the hip a bit, allowing it to be more flexible. This is an odd movement for those of you who do not know ballet! Relax with it and enjoy it. It is one of the more difficult for those who are not as flexible, but you will feel the muscles working and that's what it's all about. Do as many as you can. A good start is ten on each side.

Lie flat on your back. Slowly, with the knee facing outward, bring your toe up your calf until you reach your opposite knee. Now slowly extend the bent leg so that it is nice and straight, out to the side. You want to keep the other leg as flat to the floor as possible. To close, bring the toe back to the knee, and slide the toe back down the calf.

Lying down develop

Scissors

Unlike traditional Scissors, you will keep your legs in a turnout. This means that you will keep your heels together, but toes facing outward. If you have a bad back, it's best to keep your legs up as high as you can. If you have a strong back, keep them low. This works not only the legs, but also the lower back and lower abdomen. You'll feel this!

Start with legs in a turn out. If you have a bad back, bend your knees and open the legs so that the legs are up high. Allow one leg, than the other, to slowly move back and forth. IF you have a good back, do not extend legs upward, but start from beginning position and slowly lift one leg than the other. Don't allow your feet to touch the floor, but allow them to be just a few inches from the floor. Keeping them raised a bit off the floor gives the "resting" leg a workout too, as well as your back and abs!

Scissors

Self Improvement in terms of diet and fitness is very individual. Maybe you are thinking, "Pilates just isn't for me"—that can be true. Although I personally feel favorable about Pilates and Paivalates, there is not one activity or set of conditions that is right for everyone. As you proceed on your journey, you will see what is best for you. You will see how varied training can be. Just as I have a strong motivational edge, you will see that various trainers have strengths in other ways. Body Awareness, Nutrition, and Form—all are important. Here are a few ideas and some great free advice from a few renowned trainers from around the globe.

Aydogan, Personal Trainer

Turkey

I am a former wrestler. Fitness has been a part of my life since I was ten years old.

Crossroads
You Are Here

If people want to be in good shape and have a healthy body, they have to control all food and exercises. People do not need to go to gym. They can work from their home. My clients, I tell them that they should wake up early morning and walk or run. If not outdoors with the fresh air, then indoors on a treadmill. I also think that people should make sure they get their carbohydrates and protein, as well as a vitamin and mineral supplement.

It's all very simple. Make diet and exercise important and a priority in your life. Don't always look for the shortcuts, because the shortcuts almost always fail. It's simple. Have your goals and work towards them.

Adam Cole, USA

Guild Certified Feldenkrais® Practioner and Certified Personal Trainer www. Feldenkraisinfo.com

"Awareness of how the body works as a whole, and good organization of the skeleton, will make you much stronger and more flexible then any amount of stretching and weight-lifting will do. This is how skinny little martial artists are able to do such miraculous seeming feats."

Su Dallas-Chapman, Channel Islands

Certified Personal Trainer

"Nutrition; you will need to cut out all those extra sugars and salt. You can obtain natural salt and sugar from the foods you eat without adding extra. Vitamins and minerals are found in fresh fruit and vegetables, and you'll find plenty of protein in meats and eggs. Having lots of protein in your meals actually helps you to feel fuller for longer. You also need potatoes, wholegrain bread, fruit, vegetables and pasta to provide you with carbohydrates because without carbohydrates you cannot exercise. Your muscles gain glucose from them to use as fuel. Contrary to popular belief, carbohydrates do not make you fat, it's that funk food that contains them. It is also a good idea to take a multi-vitamin and mineral supplement to ensure that you are getting the daily-recommended amount. Drink plenty of water, a minimum of eight glasses a day. It may sound like a lot but if you add up all the other drinks you are having throughout the day, you'll be surprised. Drinking plenty of water will cleanse your system and you'll notice a big difference with your skin—it even makes a difference to those wrinkles! Water helps to plump skin, smoothing out wrinkles."

Tamir Hussain, Pakistan

Certified Personal Trainer, Master Trainer

"I have been training for ten years. The best advice I can give is; do not compromise proper form when performing an exercise. Steadily build your intensity and exercises. Don't just jump into weight training. Your body needs time to adapt. Most people want results within the first two weeks but that is the wrong approach. Also, don't underestimate the importance of diet. I feel that diet is 80% and 20% is exercise.

Sabine Berg-Swan, Bermuda

Do not ever believe that you cannot achieve your goal. Believe in yourself, think positive and the rest will come all by itself.

REST STOP

Chapter Thirteen

CROSSROAD: RELATIONSHIPS

Billboard
"But a friendship is precious not only
in the shade, but in the sunshine of life; and
thanks to a benevolent arrangement of things,
the greater part of life is sunshine"
Thomas Jefferson

RELATIONSHIPS. YOU CAN'T avoid them. For this journey, think of each relationship as someone who may be traveling with you. If you realize that one or more of these relationships are those that you really would not want to spend time with on a journey, much less a personal journey of self improvement, then you best rethink that relationship! Sometimes, relationships are just a part of being a part of society. You can't always curb the person you are with. Some relationships you have to learn to live with in some manner. In the same breath, I need to also say that empty or negative relationships are like picking up hitchhikers. You really don't need to save the world—you need to be a good person and that does not mean you have to pick up each hitchhiker who needs a ride because they don't even have a vehicle to carry them on their own journey. It's YOUR journey, so pass by the hitchhikers that are thumbing it on the side of the road. They will become baggage!

Sometimes, relationships are like a nice peaceful drive in the country, or even a scenic tour of a favorite city—you are enjoying the ride, and enjoying the passengers. Other times, you'll feel like you are in a race (perhaps at work?) or in a car derby, or playing bumper cars, such as in many family dynamics. Sometimes we feel like we are in a traffic jam—which is often the case in a more intimate relationship such as marriage.

Regardless of what relationships you want to look at (and you should be looking at most of them if not all of them right now), you need to realize a few things.

First of all, in all logic, we know for the most part that we should stand our ground, should not take abuse, not be dominated or patronized, manipulated, gilted and so on. You will hear that you should ignore what others say or do, and be comfortable in your own skin. Yes, that's true—but easier said than done.

Even the most secure person will feel twinges of insecurity if they are constantly being berated by others, especially if they are being berated by someone they either trust or admire. How do you make relationships in your life positive, more like that peaceful or scenic drive that you like?

How do you get the courage to ditch the hitchhikers you may have already picked up? You know who they are! They are the annoying "friend" who loves to "help" you when you have a crisis, but it's because she or he is so insecure that they thrive on your own insecurities and perhaps more negative issues, because it gives them self-importance. It's the wife who manipulates you or controls you. It's the boyfriend who is always borrowing money and promises to pay it back. It's parent or sibling that is always critical of you.

First, let's work on ditching the hitch-hikers so that you have more room to work on the relationships you deem most positive in your life.

It's going to be hard. Just like eating right is a time consuming for some, just like working out can be a chore—the relationship crutch, or roadblock is usually courage.

You have to think of each negative relationship that you want to ditch. One by one ask yourself what the worst case scenario would be. For most of us, it would be more that we are used to having that person around. Think of the millions of people in the world. Think of all the positive relationships of loves who have been lost—and yet, we all still go on living, finding others in the world to share the journey. So, realize that boyfriend or friend, or even sibling IS NOT air, nutrition or health. In other words, you don't

NEED them to survive. They are just another person, and bottom line, if they are not treating you with respect, you don't need them. I don't care if THEY have excuses or "issues" (their own baggage)—that is NOT your problem. They can address their own issues if they really want. No one can fix another person. Is that person drinking too much? Do they need help? Well guess what—just because YOU think they are drinking too much doesn't mean they think so—and just because YOU want them to get help (even if they say so) it is THEIR responsibility to maintain their own vehicle, fuel and all. Do you really think that your vehicle is running so smoothly that you can just sit and idle and wait? Why would you do that? Instead, to help them, be a role model. Show them how happy, healthy a person can be. Show them by example! Someone once gave me great advice. It was at a time in my life that I was feeling low, and my boyfriend was not respectful of me and actually, quite neglectful. She said, "You can love him, but you can love him from a distance." (Thank you Millie) That hit home. I realized that I did love him in my own way, but I was not getting my needs met, and it didn't look like they were going to be met anytime soon. He of course, would make promises and then they would be broken. I would live for the good days, and be heartbroken on the not so great days.

I had stayed in the relationship "working" on it—and as in many cases, the person "working" on the relationship is just failing to see that the other person is already showing you their lack of commitment by NOT working on it, so "working" on a relationship is moot, because it is one-sided. You can't be "in love" and work on a relationship if there isn't MUTUAL

LOVE. The whole idea of a relationship is that there are TWO people. You think you are in love, but you are really in a clingy stage where you live on hope, you focus on the future or the past but not the present. If the other person is not respectful, get out! Why waste your time and theirs? The non-clingy person is enjoying all the attention you are giving them, but it's all for attention sake, or from their own insecurity or whatever. This book isn't about trying to figure out what makes that person tick and making you and he or she tick-tock together, it's about you and your vehicle being happy and balanced. Would you take your car to a mechanic who promised to fix the car and then did not? Maybe once or twice, but over and over? Probably not. Maybe the first time, you'd give him the benefit of the doubt—after all, he is human and can make a mistake. But what if your car is still not running correctly and he doesn't care? He did not meet the needs of repairing the car, right? You would probably either go to another mechanic, one who will respect your needs and take time and care on your vehicle, or you will repair the car yourself. You wouldn't put up with it! Then don't do it to your self-esteem or your soul either!

Now, we all have relationships, usually that of a parent, sibling, neighbor or co-worker that are not as easy to ditch. You do not have to learn to live with their behavior. You should though, take the same basic considerations as you would if driving in hazardous conditions, or if you are on the road with a driver who is being reckless. It's really that simple. You want to stay safe, and during these situations, you are usually more alert. You are more aware of other driver's moves, more aware of how your vehicle is handling the conditions at hand—therefore, you are more prepared. You also realize that if you get into an accident, it won't be a surprise. So, do the same in these relationships. If you know your mother is going to treat you like a child in public, then perhaps you visit her only when you are going to be alone with her. Perhaps you know your co-worker is a gossip. Then, by all means, speak less to him or her—and don't disclose anything you would not want broadcasted to the office! Now, this is a touchy subject—because many men and women who are in abusive relationships are reading this and thinking, "oh, all I have to do is avoid being in public with my spouse or whomever and to avoid these issues" and the like. There is a chapter which outlines abuse in the next chapter of this book, and I suggest you read it NOW if you are in the kind of relationship that makes you feel badly, insecure, emotionally, mentally, physically or sexually abused in any way. You are not to "deal with" abusive relationships—only slightly nagging ones.

Here are some questions to help you to avoid relationship roadblocks.

Do you have anyone in your life that you dread seeing or speaking to?

Have your priorities or values changed, and yet you feel those around you have not grown?

Do you have people in your life who currently abuse you?

Souvenir: Right now, think of a positive choice in a relationship that you have made or are going to make. Think of someone in your life who has shown you respect and love. Even if you can't think of anyone, make the commitment right now, that YOU are going to be your foremost relationship with yourself. YOU will give yourself trust, respect and demand that all of the relationships in your life share the values that you put upon yourself. In the same breath, you will also be a person who gives respect—by being a friend, or in those shaky hitchhikers, by being a strong role model.

REST STOP

Chapter Fourteen

DOMESTIC ABUSE

Billboard
"He that loseth money, loseth much; he that loseth friends loseth more; but he that loseth his spirit, loseth everything"
Spanish Maxim

Hopefully, you have not been exposed to this issue, but according to statistics of many studies, many of us have been touched by the situation of domestic abuse. The issue, the crossroad, of Domestic Abuse could take up a library, let alone a single chapter. This chapter is simply to explore and raise awareness that most of the people who will be reading this book, or who even pick it up to scan it, will have, at some point in the past, present, or future, have had domestic violence touch their lives.

The reports vary, but often the numbers go as such; one in three people are touched by domestic abuse. We know that many cases of abuse go unreported, therefore the realistic number is actually probably higher than one in two, and thus, more than half of the people are victims of abuse. If more than half are victims, that means quite a large handful are also on the other end of the spectrum, being the abusers. This means, a whopping number of probably over 90% of people, are somehow involved with domestic abuse. That number is too high.

Domestic Abuse is terrorism. Terrorism in our own backyards, nursing homes, schools, bedrooms. Many people are not leading balanced lives, and are needing help to make decisions when reaching both small and large crossroads in their lives because of living or seeing abuse take place. Any child who witnesses abuse, is in fact, also abused by being exposed to it. Any adult who is abused, is carrying scars perhaps not on their skin, but always on their souls. Any abuser is often sad and confused and often frustrated—and out of control.

If you feel that you are in anyway being abused—be it by simple putdowns, sarcasm, feeling scared, feeling like you are walking on eggshells, being physically or sexually touched or harmed without consent, or being mentally or emotionally demeaned, you need to get help.

Most victims do not get help until the situations are getting out of control or until they need to flee. Most abusers do not stop—but only escalate or move to another victim. In the back of this book, there are several organizations that you can contact for help. You should do so if you feel at all that you are in danger or that you are in a relationship that is not to your benefit that you feel afraid of at any time.

If you have children and the children are seeing abuse, they are being hurt. They are victims of abuse themselves, and no matter what you say to the children, the abuse is and will continue being the norm, and they will probably either take the role of victim or abuser as an adult unless they get help. You need to take this time to get the courage, to use your vehicle, and to protect their vehicles, and take a different path. This is very important.

I was a victim of abuse. I had a pattern of non-positive relationships . . . I know what you are going through, as I have been there. I know how you pretend that everything is fine, I know you can try to fit in, but I also know you feel sad, angered, controlled, and worse yet, numb. I married someone who gave me "advice" but the advice was not two sided. He always did things "for my benefit". I soon learned that I did "nothing right" that I was "too fat" (at a size 8?) (*Even if I were overweight, it is highly abusive to tell someone that they are too fat—one should be accepted for their physical appearance and never degraded for it) . . . In a nutshell, I was berated, made to feel ashamed, guilty, I walked on eggshells. My children witnessed vulgar actions and heard vulgar language. Like you I hope, I had my breaking point. Something inside just clicks and you know you have had enough. I got a divorce. Was I confident and assure of myself?

No! I did know one thing—that it got to the point that I would rather be alone and self confident, and have peace in my home with my children than live the life I was living. I was able to keep my home, but if not, I would gladly gone to a shelter. Women (and men) DO turn their lives around and go on and live normal lives. You can turn your life around. If you contact a shelter and speak to someone you will see there are many outlets for you, to live—and to have a chance at making it to the next crossroad.

Everyone has the right to live in a home free of abuse. Terrorism of the home is not appropriate and cannot be accepted. It's up to you to make the choice. If you are an abuser, you need to make the choice to accept you have a problem and get help. Your help can be highly confidential and it is nothing to be ashamed of. It is something that you need to unlearn, and if you make it to this crossroad, you can coast slowly and pick up speed, with confidence, at being a better driver on your journey.

Are you a victim of abuse?

Do you often feel that you are being controlled, manipulated or patronized?

Do you feel you have to walk on eggshells?

Do you find yourself in situations where you are in danger, or feel you are in danger?

What can you do to stop the cycle of abuse?

Are you an abuser?

Do you often feel out of control but put on a controlled persona?

Do you need to feel macho and emotionless?

Do you have a hard time showing sorrow?

Do you ever think your actions are someone else's fault?

Do you throw things or hit, or get physically out of control?

Do you name call?

What can you do to change some of your actions?

Do you have the courage to seek help?

Souvenir: Imagine that you are you, but without abuse in your life. Imagine that you are with someone; even your present spouse, friend, family member, and they are not abusive/victims. How does this make you feel? Imagine yourself getting help—imagine that people are there to help you. There are.

REST STOP

Chapter Fifteen

CROSSROAD: SPIRITUALITY

Billboard
"It is more blessed to give than to receive"
Acts, 20:35

F OR MANY OF us, Spirituality is non-existent in our lives, or perhaps something we "do" rather than feel. In almost all religions or avenues of meditation, the basis of spirituality is that something is within us.

Spirituality can be, but is not always, religion. Religion is a structured base of worship, usually within a structured group following guidelines or rules, such as the Catholic religion or Scientology.

Spirituality can be found in religions of course, and often is; but it is also a very personal self-faith, deep within our souls, which, because of the personalization, can be very different for each person. It is sometimes what gives us strength, what gives us hope. It can be that time we devote to our inner selves, and the place within us in which we strive for perfection, for all things good, and for positive enrichment.

Spirituality is important, because it gives us a base. It's like the garage for our vehicle. Somewhere to go to, to rest, to fuel up, to be maintained. It's the place where we can be ourselves.

If you have a hard time finding your spiritual self, you should look to different religions. Many people stay with the religion that perhaps they were taught and brought up with as a child. Some people never have religion in their lives until they reach adulthood, and some people study different religions and pull the parts they admire and feel comfortable with from each one.

Becoming a part of a religious group gives not only a set of boundaries and values to guide yourself to, but it comes complete with a support system of people, study, worship and various extended groups that often extend beyond the religious studying. For instance, many times churches have youth groups, singles groups, sports teams and outreach groups. These groups may have nothing more to do with the religion itself other than the group of people within these extensions all have the common thread of belonging to the same structured religion and house of worship.

If you are more interested in exploring your inner spirituality without the structure of a religion, there are many ways to do so. You could do the obvious and research through the library or Internet. You could also do something as simple as live by a motto or creed that you have heard and admire or have made up yourself that is both positive and life enriching. Another thing you can do to boost your spirituality is to continue to broaden and live by self-made guidelines for living.

When you have spirituality in your life, you often have a stronger sense of who you are. It's because among other things that religion or spirituality have to offer (regardless of your beliefs), having spirituality is like standing up for yourself and your thoughts. It is an additional inner-fuel for your vehicle.

One aspect of truly being spiritual is that you do not cast judgement on others. If you are religious without spirituality, one sometimes can become judgmental. If many as a group share this trait, the group as a whole believes that only their set of beliefs is valid and does not respect other's beliefs. The goal on your journey, as to also create an inner peace within yourself, is to accept others for who they are spiritually.

If you cannot be at peace with those around you, it is likely that you will not be at peace with yourself. When one is spiritual, one realizes that what works for you may not work for someone else, and likewise.

As you become more spiritual, and explore spiritual outlets, you will begin to focus more on your own spiritual awakenings, and less on the spiritual practices, customs and traditions of others.

Part of your journey you will realize is to share the road with others, but control only your own vehicle.

Keeping a strong hold on your spirituality will help you stay on the right path, and when you come to a crossroad, it will be easier to make those decisions every day because you will be building a set of guidelines that strengthen each time you reach down within. Your spirituality will help you to become more internal, and less external. It will give you protection and guidance.

What memories, if any, do you have of spirituality in your life?

What is something that is very important to you?

In what ways do you think a stronger spiritual life would have helped you in past decisions?

What are ways that you can explore spirituality in your life today?

Do you have at least one person, right now, that can help you in your spiritual quest?

If you are alone on your spiritual quèst, do you have a plan in which to begin?

Souvenir: Picture yourself at a very peaceful place. Imagine there is no hate, no envy, and no hardship. There is peace, there is love. Imagine that feeling within you—and realize that it is there. It is always there. If you can imagine it now, you have it within you. You just need to refine yourself a bit, and make this place more prevalent in your everyday life. Soon, you will see that no matter where you are on your map, you are really always at this wondrous place of spirituality.

REST STOP

Chapter sixteen

CROSSROAD: STRESS MANAGEMENT

Billboard
"Do not anticipate trouble, or worry about what may never happen. Keep in the sunlight."
Benjamin Franklin

ON YOUR JOURNEY, there will be cars, mopeds, trucks and vehicles of all kinds in front of you, behind you, next to you. Some will cut you off, some will speed, some will be broken down on the side of the road, some will tailgate, some will be getting tickets, some will be noisy . . . there will be a lot to deal with on the road, and you have to deal with it. You need to find a way to manage your stress. Stress can tax the body and zap your energy, your zest for life and create health and mental issues.

It's easier said than done when you hear someone

telling you to just "relax". Some of us look relaxed on the outside, but we know we feel nervous or anxious. Some of us claim to be "totally calm" while we grind our teeth, have frequent headaches and so on . . . and some of us, like myself, just plain admit that "Yes, sometimes stress can get the better of me!"

Stress affects us in many ways. It affects our mind, our body and of course, the way in which we react and act.

One thing stressed people tend to do is overreact. Have you ever felt so on edge, with the anxiety accumulating after months, days or perhaps even minutes? Overreaction snowballs, because the person we overreact with usually gets defensive and surprise—overreacts with us too. We get angry, carry around the feelings of frustration and anger, and our next wave of anxiety builds again within us. It can make us feel jittery, anxious, unhappy, depressed or even bitter and vindictive.

One thing that you will notice is that oftentimes when we "overreact" it is because we are almost responding from reflex. When we see a stressful situation coming our way, we regress back to old habits, old patterns of behavior. It's easy to feel stressed not only from the situation itself, but from realizing that you have overreacted. You have to think of this as skidding on a slick road . . . just get back on course, and drive safely. It's really that simple. The less we beat ourselves up for regressing to old habits, the less importance we give those old habits too. The less importance they have, the less we think about them, and the less we have them.

Overreacting is just one way we store stress.

How often do you say the following?

I should have . . .

I could have . . . .

I ought to have . . .

I ought to . . . .

I wish I didn't . . . .

There are many more phrases and negative words that people use when they think to themselves that are creating a cycle of stress. This stress is coming from the core of not being able to feel good about themselves, not feeling like they are good enough to measure up to others or what others want in them and perhaps even just an overall negative outlook. You have to be able to jump back quickly—put your vehicle in reverse, and think about the perception you are building in your mind. You don't even realize you are doing it!

Ask yourself these questions.

Am I really not good enough?

Does this person's opinion really matter in the scheme of things?

Am I maybe jumping to conclusions about myself?

Am I a pretty good person overall?

Hopefully, if you can reverse and think about these questions, you will see that you really don't have to "should all over yourself"!

Another tactic you can use is to just stop and breathe. This sounds simple, right? You are breathing all day and all night! You don't need anyone to actually tell you to breathe! Well, guess what. It's actually harder than you think. When I say to stop and Breathe, I mean, really stop what you are doing. Just stop. Stop arguing, stop feeling impatient in the grocery line, stop the meeting that you are holding. STOP. Then, concentrate on your breathing. Chances are, your heart rate will be elevated a bit due to stress and your breathing will be more shallow. You need to slow the breathing down. Inhale deeply and as you do, clear your thoughts so that you are really just thinking about your slow inhale. Make sure you inhale through your nose if you can. Then, slowly exhale through your mouth. Really let the air blow past your lips and outward. Feel the stress leaving your body a bit at a time. Think only about your breathing. Chances are you will be also thinking more positive thoughts because you will be calming yourself down and you won't be getting caught up in overreacting and acting on impulse or reaction. You have done a great thing... you've gained control of your vehicle.

I'm here to tell you from experience, cut off stress before it cuts you off!

REST STOP

My Own Stress Story

Let me first tell you a little about my own stress. First, there I was in that poor relationship—you know, the one where I overate? Well, I was also stressed out. Crying easily, easily frustrated, angered and on edge. I was working out a little, but nothing major. I was still overeating and still trying to live on hope with that relationship, not reality! So, there I was, having teeth problems. I'd go to the dentist, and he would say, "do you grind your teeth?" and I would say, "no" and he would say, "Yes you do." But I did not think I did, therefore, I thought he was a nut! My excuse was that he was a doctor just trying to make more money off of me. Wrong! I was grinding my teeth, and I did not realize this until a least a year later, and I did finally get fitted with an mouthpiece to wear at night that would both help me break the habit and add comfort to my aching teeth and jaws. Now, right after this point, my mother discovered she had cancer. Around that time, I started having heart palpitations—and I swore I was having a heart attack! Here I was, in my late twenties, with a seemingly ok life, two kids, a nice home, a thriving business (dance studio) and plenty of friends . . . so I thought that there was no way that I could be under any severe stress, so it must be a heart problem. I had numerous trips to the emergency room thinking I was having a heart attack. I visited the doctor's office. I even had to wear a heart monitor for a couple of days to monitor my heart. Well, after testing after testing, the only answer was STRESS. I was fine. The medical professionals told me that my heart was in great condition.

OK—mind you, I was in my little denial world that my

marriage was great—and because it was a verbally and emotionally abusive marriage, I felt insecure, yet, that if I "just shaped up" and "stopped being so horrible" that my "heart" problems would go away. It wasn't only heart symptoms, which were scary and real. But also other things, like frequent colds, feeling tired, feeling jumpy—the full spectrum of symptoms that would make those around me fear that I was a hypochondriac. In reality, it was all real, it was simply stress-induced. Doctors recommended I exercise. I started really slowly—as I was afraid that my heart might give out (I wasn't convinced it was stress). After a while, I realized I wasn't going to have a heart attack. Of course, I was still stressed, but going to the gym made me feel better. The endorphins that are released as you exercise are natural mood enhancers, and also the physical act of working out strengthens and works your body. Palpitations from stress are due to an overabundance of adrenaline, and working out uses that adrenaline so that your body doesn't have the "overdose" of it that causes stress related issues, such as those palpitations.

Along the way, after a divorce and my mother's death, I learned that I am much stronger than I thought emotionally, and that anyone can overcome stress if they put their mind to it. It's all about making it a priority—and I want you to make stress reduction a priority. But you have to do it your way . . . what works for one person does not work always for another.

I was told countless times to try Yoga. I have tried several Yoga classes. The slower Yoga that is so relaxing to many is just annoying to me! Yoga is great for many, but it's not, as my mother used to say, "my cup of tea". So, when exploring stress reduction techniques, explore, but do what is right for you, not for your friend or your neighbor. This is your journey, and only you are driving your vehicle.

REST STOP

Ways To Relax

Here are some wonderful way's to relax. Usually, it's best to combine many forms because depending upon your mood, one or the other may work best, such as meditation, having a hobby, sports, listening to music and so on.

Hobbies

Take something and be passionate about it. This will help you to focus on something other than your stress. It helps if you have a variety of hobbies. This way, you have active hobbies (those that are more physical and spontaneous) such as painting, cooking, playing music—and inactive hobbies (those which you collect, admire or share) such as stamp collecting, flea-marketing, reading)

A combination of hobbies also makes you appreciate other's hobbies and then you are more open to learning thus begin to focus more on positive aspects rather than sit around dwelling on negative ones.

My husband and I have a ton of hobbies, many of

which we share. Our shared hobbies include gardening, flea-marketing, writing, reading, looking at old movies, collecting antique toys, listening to a variety of music, art, crafts and more. Some hobbies are not shared, but complimentary, such as I design items and he makes them in his workshop. Other hobbies are not shared at all, such as my collection of "I dream of Jeannie" memorabilia and his obsession with shipwrecks. The bottom line is, with all of this, and more that I didn't even mention; we have a lot of outlets for stress. We also don't get critical with our hobbies at all—it's all for fun, nothing is taken too seriously, and we are happy for each other when we get new hobbies.

Most times stress comes from an unbalance. If you feel you are stressed because you don't have time, you better find a way to make time. I hear a lot of homemakers say that they don't have time. What they mean is they don't make time. We all have the same 24 hours. Some of us are complaining we don't have time; others of us are stars of movies, and still spending time with our children. Some of us are doctors saving lives, and still have time to research theories on curing cancer and still have time to go to the school play of our preschooler. Don't make excuses. Just make time. If you feel you don't have enough money, then get a hobby that doesn't cost much or cost anything. Collect leaves. Find the beauty in something, find the passion in something. If you can't find passion, then you have to search deeper inside of yourself. If you are bored by life, you are really bored with yourself. If your view from your vehicle is boring or too stressful, then it's time to change lanes, get off the highway and take another route.

Exercise

OK, you may not want to hear this but exercise is a wonderful stress reducer. You need to check with your physician first, but moving is a key in feeling better. If you have a bad back or limited mobility, you should try something like Pilates, or a gentle Yoga class. Swimming is also something that does not stress the joints much. If you are fairly strong without health issues, running, weightlifting and cross training are great ways to beat the blahs. Remember that sports are not exactly exercise. If you are out of shape, playing tennis is a hobby. It's the training before the sport that is actually better for you—but if you like sports, you should try to fit both in, as to avoid injury during the game. All serious athletes—from baseball to tennis, do more than just play the game you see on TV. They train. They train to get in shape, stay fit, avoid injury, perfect their game, and perfect their stamina. You should too!

Above all, stress reduction is all about doing things to make you happier and more balanced in your life.

What do you do to relax now?

What are things you would like to do that you would find relaxing?

Do you carry the stress in your neck (pains) Stomach (upset stomach) or in other physical areas?

If so, what can you do to minimize these symptoms before they start?

Was there a time in your life where you felt fairly unstressed? If so, what about that time can you recreate?

Is there a support group at your local hospital that helps people with dealing with stress?

Souvenir: Imagine all the possibilities for your life. Imagine all the things you'd like to learn about. Try imagining yourself doing something out of character that you'd love to do . . . then do it.

REST STOP

Chapter Seventeen

AROMATHERAPY—

AROMATHERAPY IS GREAT. Aromatherapy is a wonderful hobby, a great way to de-stress and sometimes can have medicinal benefits. Aromas are our link to communicating by scent, by breathing. Smell is one of the first senses that was developed while we were just a small form, without arms or legs. Our brains began as two bumps on the olfactory stalks, therefore, we smelled long before we heard, tasted or even saw a thing. Aromatic chemistry, aromatherapy and other aroma techniques have all been born, or reborn, because we humans have realized that the sense of smell is a very powerful thing. I am not an Aromatic Chemist, but I am a follower of aromatherapy, so for all intensive purposes, we will leave the intricate designs to the study of chemical aroma to the chemists, and we will just talk about the fun stuff!

Aroma is an integral part of attraction and allure, and even marketing executives know that smell is a major sales tool. There are many perfumes and even the bottled attraction called Pheromones. Humans start secreting pheromones at puberty, and some think that this is to alert the opposite sex to reproductive readiness. We will get into some essential oils, which mimic or bring out, the much talked about pheromones too!

One of my hobbies is making Aromatherapy Spritzers. I love to blend oils and discover which little blend works best for this or that, or think of how one aroma makes me feel as opposed to another. I like to make them, and then give them silly names. I made one for my sister, who was having some peri-menapausel-like symptoms, and called it "Crazy Lady". Back to the subject! Aromatherapy works. You need not go deep into as I did, blending oils and such, but you can buy a nice aroma candle. Often the aroma of the candle coupled with the look of the flickering flame can calm you down a bit . . . it's a great way to wind down after a hard day of work, or a lazy day where you may be thinking "too much" about the less splendid events of the day, month or year. Aromatherapy can also take the form of fresh flowers, baking bread, or just the smell of play dough. Anything that gives you a good feeling by scent is aromatherapy. The best way to find the scent that you enjoy is to try a variety. For me, eucalyptus is my favorite choice for a candle. Although some say it is invigorating, I find it calms me down and chases stress away.

Do not ever use essential oils unless you know how to

do so. Most essential oils are too strong to be used by themselves, and can even burn the skin. Make sure you speak to someone before mixing oils. If you are a beginner, it is best to utilize a company that already makes aromatherapy products that are diluted and safe, that you can sample, such as Burts Bees that carries a Carrot Seed Oil spray that I love. Here are some samples of oils and their physical and emotional uses that they are commonly used for.

Carrot Seed Oil

This is a sweet scent, and is often used on mature or sun-damaged skin. Emotionally, it can create a revitalization of energy.

Chamomile

This is a deep rich scent, and is often used to lessen anxiety emotionally, while physically it is said to induce sleep. This is the herb that is used as a tea.

Ginger

This is a sweet, sharp scent, and is used as a muscular anti-spasmodic. Emotionally, this is said to aid in confidence building.

Lemon

Lemon is a sharp, bright scent. It is known for it's anti-viral and decongestant abilities and it is said that the scent of it triggers clear thoughts, trust and cleanings (think of how many cleaning products have a "fresh lemon scent"!)

Peppermint

This is a nice, minty scent. Emotionally, it stimulates the mind, develops emotional tolerance and physically is said to help the respiratory and digestive systems.

Rose

The rose has a sensual scent. It is thought to banish jealousy and trigger deeper love. Physically it is said to help curb premenstrual and female hormonal symptoms.

Here are some of the scents that give sensual thoughts to some!

Sandalwood

A soft, earthy fragrance. *This is one of those that mimic's pheromones!*

Patchouli

A rich, woodsy fragrance *this is one of those that mimic's pheromones!*

Lavender

A light fragrance with a sweet tone.

This is just a hint of what essential oils are available, and just a peek at what their many uses can be directed towards.

Remember that essential oils can be dangerous, and

you could have severe allergies to the oils. It is always best to check with an aroma therapist or even an allergist before using the oils. The oils can have very strong scents and can cause allergic reactions even to those who live with you. Also, never, ever ingest the oils. For the most part, they are pure topical ointments and spirtzers.

What are some scents that remind you of childhood?

Is there someone in your life, or was there, that had a scent that you just could inhale all day?

What is a fond memory that is sometimes triggered by a scent for you?

REST STOP

Chapter Eighteen

BEAUTY FOR EVERYONE, NATURALLY

Billboard
"People are like stained glass windows, beautiful when the sun shines on them, With their true beauty coming from within"
Elizabeth Kubler Ross

BEFORE WE EVEN delve into this subject, let me tell you that we need to talk again about "perception". We often look into the mirror and do not like the beautiful or handsome face we see. We see scars, blemishes, distorted features and so on. But what you should be seeing is that amazing miracle that is you. We are all beautiful—every man, woman and child. You need to change your perception so that you do not look at yourself and find yourself looking "down" on yourself. You need to again reach down and grab some confidence and swallow it like you mean it... and mean it! That being said, let's not look to change you, but to improve what you've got. Your package, what the outside world looks at, what you look at when you look in the mirror, is the external stuff. When you look good, it's hard to feel bad. When you make great choices when you come to your crossroads, you should reward yourself with pampering yourself daily. Here are some great all natural tips, advice and theories that you can use.

Herbal After-Shave for Men

This is a great after-shave that will not only wake up your senses, but is all natural.

Combine a half-cup of vodka, two drops of patchouli, three drops of rosemary, two drops of sage and one drop of peppermint. Combine with a cup of witch hazel. Mix well, and use. The vodka acts as a preservative and you can keep this up to one month.

Facial Skincare

Note that the following "recipes" are topical and not to be ingested!

Oily Skin—Yogurt is great for oily skin. It's best to not add an essential oil to the yogurt if you do have oily or combination skin. Make sure you are using a plain yogurt without added sugars. Sugar grows bacteria easily and is that last thing you want on oily skin, which usually traps bacteria! You can add the contents to a vitamin E capsule to the yogurt if you want to try to get some topical anti-oxidant, and you can add lemon juice if you'd like to lightly bleach sunspots. Lemon also helps fight acne.

Dry Skin—Sour Cream is wonderful for dry skin. You will feel your skin seem more elastic and appear younger looking. You can add several drops of carrot seed oil to the sour cream and mix well. This will also ease sun stressed skin.

Facial Scrub—mix 4 tablespoons dry oatmeal or oats, one egg, one-teaspoon oil (olive oil is preferred) and one tablespoon of honey. Mix and apply onto the face for about fifteen minutes. Rinse off and splash cider vinegar mixture (see below) as a toner.

Toner—mix a quarter cup of cider vinegar, a quarter cup of witch hazel, and a splash of lemon juice together. Apply on face and pat dry with towel.

Body Skincare

Dry Skin—Olive Oil is a great skin softener. To really get the full benefit, simply warm the olive oil a bit and apply after it cools so that it is comfortable to the touch. Allow it to soak into the skin and as it does, reapply again. You can put one drop of an essential oil, such as lavender, rose, sandalwood—or oil of your choice, with it to add a more pleasant scent.

Blemishes—A blemish is always an unpleasant guest on your face or body. To get rid of this unwanted guest, dry it out with cider vinegar, alcohol, white wine or lemon juice. Make sure you just use a cotton ball and avoid getting the astringent into your eyes.

Oily Hair—rinse with cider vinegar

Dry Hair—rinse with a mixture of two cups of water, three drops rosemary oil.

To really keep your hair in great condition, apply olive oil to the hair. If your hair is oily, apply only to the ends. After applying, wrap hair in a towel for at least a half hour. Rinse. Your hair will be shiny and look healthy!

For more Body—Allow a can of beer to go flat. Rinse hair, after shampooing, with this flat beer. Your hair will be full of bounce!

Balding—I really don't know if this works, but I was told that rubbing any stimulating essential oil into the skin, such as carrot seed oil, will boost circulation and keep balding at bay. A country friend also told me that rubbing an onion on the scalp would ward off baldness. My guess is it would ward off just about anything, including loved ones! Phew!

To increase the intensity of hair color, add the following oils to two cups of water and rinse.

Blonde Hair—Chamomile, Turmeric

Brown Hair—Cinnamon, Cloves

Red Hair—Henna, Juniper Berry

Black Hair—Walnut, Elder Leaves

One thing to be aware of when speaking of beauty is that your idea of beauty and someone else's idea can be very different.

For instance, I wholeheartedly enjoy make-up. I wear make-up most of the time. My girlfriend Sue can't stand make-up and barely ever wears it. My idea of looking "fresh faced" is just a touch of lipstick. Her idea of "made-up" is just a touch of lipstick. So, you need to remember this if you are fine-tuning your vehicle along with a friend, so to say. What works for him or her, may not work for you. Remember that it's your vehicle and that you should do what feels right for you.

Your vehicle, your package, is all about what feels good on you, to you. What you look like and how you present yourself is your presentation package. Your looks, your body language, expressions . . . all of this goes into how you appear to others, and perhaps how you feel about yourself. There are some basics about presenting yourself that go way beyond the color lipstick you wear, or the type of tie you choose on any particular day.

Do you slouch? Slouching is one of the biggest killers of presentation. Slouching makes you look insecure, lazy or even heavier. It may make you look uninterested or uncaring. Now, you may be saying "but I am insecure and quite honestly, maybe even lazy too!"—well, that's fine. The world doesn't need to know that. You are working (I hope) on remedying the fact that you may be insecure or lazy, and soon you won't feel that way. But the sooner you stop the habit of slouching—and it does become a habit quickly, the sooner you will appear more secure, more alert. You will probably feel better too once you begin to stop that habit, because when your posture is nice and erect, your breathing will be much more thorough as well, thus giving you an increase in oxygen, and in the long run, probably energy too.

When you talk to people, do you not look at them in the eye? That is another big presentation killer. This makes you less attractive because it makes you seem not interested, and perhaps even insecure. Worse yet, it makes you seem a bit shady and distrustful. Not good. You need to learn—practice with your best friend, your spouse, your own image in the mirror—even with your cat or dog if you have to. But LOOK at the other person (or animal!) while you speak to them. Really concentrate on looking at the bank teller or grocer or whomever. Be interested in others and try to really take notice of their body language and facial expressions. This little "job" will help you to train yourself to look at the other person, thus, create a more attractive you.

Do you want to know another "beauty" tip that is really a *presentation* tip? One that will also shape the *way others see you?*

It's the handshake.

A handshake is a tricky thing. First of all, you should always extend your hand for a handshake. Don't always wait to be reply to the handshake. Extending your hand (in American Culture) represents both respect and authority. It shows you care about the other person, even if on a business level, and that you respect not only them, but also yourself. It gives an appearance of security too, because you are not cowering back from the shake, but initiating it. When you shake, don't do what some call the "dead fish", which is very limp. Many women do this shake, and I suppose because they feel it's feminine, they continue with it.I personally, think regardless of if you are a male or female, it just seems plain wimpy. Listen; if you are a woman, it's probably no secret. I don't think you have to prove it by shaking hands like a dead fish, so don't. More than likely, the dead-fish shake just makes you look insecure, wimpy or even like a bimbo. Get tougher! On another note, don't get too tough. Don't do the grab where you squeeze the life out of the other person. That can look like you want to control them, or that you are trying to convince them of something. Unless the handshake is meant to be very intimate, I wouldn't grab the other person with the other hand while you are doing the handshake. Some people are ok with this, but some people will feel like you are invading their space or being unprofessional. All in all, a nice firm handshake where you let go after a maximum of two "shakes" would be appropriate.

Beauty isn't always about looking perfect.

How often have you known someone who initially you thought was not that attractive, but all of a sudden, after knowing them, they seemed more attractive? That's because their inner beauty shone through to you. I have met very beautiful people, make and female, who actually became less attractive to me because they either had developed poor habits, poor social skills or just were not very genuine people. It's all about who you are on the inside. I'm sure that some of you reading this wanted some magic answers on how to apply the perfect makeup, or get your beard to maintain that perfect five O clock shadow all day. Maybe now you realize that make-up and beard growth matter less than being confident in who you are—even without make-up or with a bit of overgrown beard. Beauty really is who you are. The other stuff is just topical. Beauty also comes and goes, styles and trends may be fickle from one day to the next, but if you are confident in who you are—no matter what your age or what crossroad you are coming to on your map, you will always be beautiful or handsome. Sappy, but true!

Who do you think is the most beautiful person you know? Why?

What can you do to make yourself more handsome or beautiful to your loved ones? To yourself?

Think of a time in your life where you felt the most attractive. Why did you feel that way?

Do you often look to others for your acceptance of your attractiveness? How can this backfire on you?

What is beautiful about you, right now?

REST STOP

Chapter Nineteen

THE ONGOING JOURNEY
THAT WE CALL "LIFE"

Billboard
"Growth is the only evidence of life"
Cardinal Newman

HOPEFULLY, YOU ARE working on your major crossroads, and hopefully this book can be the beginning of your map, or plan to help you achieve your goals and set you on a road of personal success, whatever that personal success is for you.

For most of us, it will be a complex road, because there are many area's that find we need to slow down, stop, and tune up. We sometimes drive for miles, only to notice the fuel light is on—or we neglect ourselves and find we are breaking down and in need of repair. But once we start to make better decisions, and better choices as we come to our crossroads, we will find fewer moments of confusion, uncertainty and insecurity.

As we proceed on our journeys, and proceed forward without running in circles or stuck in a traffic jam, will begin to feel the joy as we see the open road before us. We feel the air brush our cheeks as we roll along taking with us souvenirs and learning as we go. We will meet people and forge relationships, we will overcome those who we before allowed to empower us, and we will feel strong and healthy. We will be able to look into our rearview mirrors and smile at the person we see, and we will have our hands firmly planted on the steering wheel, and we will know that we are in fact, the person in the drivers seat.

Throughout my life, I have had many changes take place. I've been at many crossroads. I've been in positions where I was afraid to take a chance, afraid to live. I've had stress overcome me so much I did not want to go to a store, or feared that I was having a heart attack. I've also learned a lot of lessons. Some who have been in similar situations may still be there. Maybe you are reading this; maybe you are in an abusive marriage with little ones who you are trying to protect. Maybe you look, as I did, at sleeping children and whisper that someday it was going to be better. But like me perhaps, you did not know how, only that you wanted it. It may have seemed like a distant wish, but one you wish would come true. Maybe you just want to lose ten pounds, maybe your crossroad is you want to quit your job and stay home with your children. Maybe your crossroad it that you want to be more loving to your wife, or that you want to spend more time with your siblings who you lost touch with. Regardless of where you were, you are here, now.

You can begin to make little changes, because I did, and those little changes become a series of changes, and a series of changes becomes a lifestyle change, and that becomes a change in your life. If you develop self-confidence—and it will be slow, not overnight—and learn to get in touch with what your vehicle really is and where it wants to really go, you will see that crossroads are something to embrace, not fear or be bothered by.

Several years ago, I was sitting on my mother's couch in her home, with my sister on her other side . . . she was very ill, in the last stages of cancer, dying at home with dignity with the aid of the Hospice program. We held her and cried, and we told her it was ok to die, ok to let go, that we would love, and we loved her forever. She died January 4th . . . . My divorce was finalized that same year. That same year, I met my present husband, my soul mate, and my best friend. I realized life is too short. I continued to lose the extra weight, to tone up, to concentrate on me, and my vehicle. I realized I was chunky (not fat, just chunky) because I was hiding myself. I was afraid to be me. I entered, and won, the title of Mrs. Pennsylvania 2002. To be honored with the Crown of Mrs. PA International has been yet another crossroad. It has taught me so much. It's not about competing with others, but competing with oneself. When you compete with yourself, you are always the victor. Even if you think you have not succeeded at a goal, you are closer to the goal if nothing else. Holding the title of Mrs. Pennsylvania International has helped me to further my understanding of volunteerism, and the gravity that a person can accomplish to help those in need. The pageant itself is a non-exploitive organization, which promotes strong, committed married relationships, and the joys family life brings. The great people I have met through this system have also taught me that regardless of if you are married or single, you can embrace those virtues and become a much more balanced person. And like any vehicle, if you are balanced, you are probably running at your peak.

So, here I sit, writing this, and feeling that I'm on top of the world—and yet, if you knew the struggles I have had, the nights at the hospital during an abusive marriage, the nights looking at my children hoping for a better life, the days holding my mother while she slowly died, and the day I held my father-in-laws hand as he passed away.... it seems like so long ago, but like yesterday. All of these experiences were horrible—yet beautiful. All taught me about strength, love, and about myself. I have been at so many crossroads, so many at once that I've felt lost. It took a lot of little risks, a lot of little decisions, but slowly, I was back on the right track. I'm happy that I've had the upheavals that I did, because I sincerely

Crossroads
You Are Here

feel that I am stronger and wiser because of them. We all have had upheavals, and we all know sorrow. We've all come to some big crossroads and for the most part, we will all experience more crossroads along our journey as well . . . it's what you do when you get to the crossroads that matter.

My girlfriend has a daughter, Julia, who has a myriad of health problems. Julia is just six years old, has a feeding tube, doesn't speak, doesn't communicate, can't walk or sit up on her own, and has seizures almost weekly. Julia though, has brought so much to so many. She can glance into your eyes, and your heart melts. Anyway, the point is, Julia has a nurse that visits the home several times a week, and this nurse, Shirley, has become an extended part of their family.

One day recently, I really got to know Shirley more. I always knew she was a nice and genuine person . . . . she has a great sense of humor, and we can sit down and talk and laugh. You are always assured of laughing when Shirley is around. The other day though, as I said, I really got to know her more. She was talking to Sue and I about how happiness is really within you, not external at all. She meets a lot of different families as a home care nurse, and she is subjected to a varying amount of emotions as each family has different, sometimes negative, mechanics.

But Shirley has a very strong spiritual side and a strong grasp of where she is in life . . . basically; she is in a secure vehicle, with a nice clear map of where she is going. She doesn't have a ton of baggage, and she is confident that no matter what crossroad she will come to, she will be able to handle herself safely through the journey. She has had her share of crossroads in her life, with a divorce and being a single mother. She has had pain, and she has cried—but she has also put those windshield wipers on, brushed off those tears, and saw the road in front of her was there for her to travel. Shirley is the perfect example of a person who is on the right road.

You are your own vehicle, and you are the only one who can say what is right for you. Only you know where you want to go in life, and even if you don't have long-term goals, you can feel more confident with the smaller crossroads that you come to.

There is no excuse for abuse. There is no excuse for being unfit. There is no excuse for eating poorly. There is no reason to carry extra baggage that just wears you down. There is no excuse to not write your feelings down and face them. There is no excuse to be insecure.

You can empower yourself.

Now is the time—you are here.

Resources

The Family Violence Prevention Fund
383 Rhode Island Street, Suite 304
San Francisco, CA 94103-5133
www.fvpf.org

Mrs. International Pageant, Inc
P.O. Box 12426
Roanoke, Virginia 24025
www.mrsinternational.com

Silenttears.org
An online resource

ACNTV.com
for your jewelry & collectable needs

Personal Distance Coaching

You can have personal distance coaching
with Michele Paiva!
We will discuss your physical and nutritional crossroads,
as well as help to pave a customized path for you.
The ongoing sessions will enable us to work together as
you achieve your goals, and encourage you
if you find yourself struggling or in a setback.
You must call first to set up your appointment time.
We do offer a varied schedule for your
convenience and budget.
Call or email for prices and information.
MicheleMPaiva@aol.com

Email me if you are entering a pageant
and are interested!

Upcoming workbook, "Spiritual Fitness" underway!
Spiritual Fitness: A guide for the Body and Soul

WORKOUT VIDEO—NEED REAL PEOPLE WITH A SENSE OF HUMOR!
We are putting together a video workout!

CROSSROADS
YOU ARE HERE

If you would like to be considered
for the work-out, email me at
MicheleMPaiva@aol.com

UPCOMING BOOK NEEDS YOUR CROSSROADS STORY!

Would you like your story to be included in an
upcoming book? We are looking for people
to talk about their most major crossroad
thus far. What in your life was a changing point?
Tell us how you did it, and what you learned
from that experience.

Please email your story, no more than 2,000 words
(we reserve the right to edit) to Michele at
MicheleMPaiva@aol.com

Coming soon! Our website! (MichelePaiva.Com)

Here you will find advice on your many crossroads
and a variety of items to help you on your journey.
Sign up for our mailing list and get insider news,
discounts and more!

BALLETSA, Inc

The word "Balletsa" many people think pertains to dance, as much of my life was influenced by dance.

The name is actually a phonetic spelling of an Italian word meaning "Sweetheart". My mother was Italian and used to call me her "Balletsa" . . . . it was her love that inspired so much in my life, and naming my company "Balletsa" is just one of the many ways of always keeping her close to me.

Printed in the United States
20318LVS00001B/335